Turn Left at the Pub

**Twenty Walking Tours Through
the British Countryside**

George W. Oakes

with new and additional research material by
Anton Powell

Turn Left at the Pub

Fourth Edition

An Owl Book

Henry Holt and Company
New York

Henry Holt and Company, Inc.
Publishers since 1866
115 West 18th Street
New York, New York 10011

Henry Holt® is a registered
trademark of Henry Holt and Company, Inc.

Published in Canada by Fitzhenry & Whiteside Ltd.,
195 Allstate Parkway, Markham, Ontario L3R 4T8.

First published 1968 by David McKay Company, Inc., New York
First paperback edition published by Congdon & Weed, Inc.,
298 Fifth Avenue, New York, NY 10001

Library of Congress Cataloging-in-Publication Data
Oakes, George W., 1909–1965.
    Turn left at the pub: twenty walking tours through
the British countryside / George W. Oakes;
with new and additional research material
by Anton Powell.—4th ed., 1st Owl Book ed.
        p.   cm.
"An Owl book."
    ISBN 0-8050-3860-4 (pbk.: alk. paper)
    1. Walking—Great Britain—Guidebooks.   2. Great Britain—Tours.
  I. Powell, Anton.   II. Title.
DA650.028   1998   97-26831
914.104'859—dc21   CIP

Henry Holt books are available for special promotions
and premiums. For details contact: Director, Special Markets.

First Owl Book Edition 1998

DESIGNED BY BETTY LEW

Printed in the United States of America
All first editions are printed on acid-free paper. ∞

10   9   8   7   6   5   4   3   2   1

Contents ⚘

Editor's Note	*vii*
Bath I	*3*
Bath II	*12*
Cambridge I	*17*
Cambridge II	*29*
Canterbury	*37*
Chichester	*48*
Church Stretton	*58*
Dorchester	*67*
Hay-on-Wye	*77*
Knole	*86*
Oxford I	*95*
Oxford II	*108*
St. David's and Solva	*113*

Salisbury	*124*
Stow-on-the-Wold	*133*
Tenby	*141*
Wells	*150*
York I	*158*
York II	*167*
Index	*173*

Editor's Note ✦

The key to maximum enjoyment of this book is a little advance planning. It is a good idea to read through the walks before you start out. In some cases, such as the country walks, you may find you have just walked straight through the lunch hour. As most pubs and small restaurants close at two o'clock, it is a good idea to take a picnic lunch or be sure to finish the walk before closing time.

Museums and national monuments have a tendency to change their hours frequently, so if there is a place of particular interest you want to see, we recommend you doublecheck the hours before starting out. It is a good idea to check bus schedules and available taxi services before you do a country walk, in case you should want to return the easy way.

The shoes you wear for rural walks should be comfortable and reasonably water-resistant. The soles should *not* be leather and should be non-skid—the rougher the sole (short of cleats) the better.

Slacks are most practical for ladies. And no matter how sunny the day, you will never regret carrying a rolled up raincoat or poncho.

Thirteen of the twenty walks are the combined work of Oakes and Powell. Powell alone wrote the following: "Church Stretton," "Dorchester," "Hay-on-Wye," "Knole," "St. David's and Solva," and "Tenby."

Turn Left at the Pub

BATH I ☙

Bath is perhaps the prettiest town in Britain. The Romans made the
site famous across Europe for its hot spring. The elaborate ruins of
the **Roman swimming pool** and **bath house** are now jewels, to com-
pare with Stonehenge or York Minster. But the town of Bath is
more than an elegant setting. In the 1700s it became the favorite
place of the grandees of England. Top politicians, soldiers, writers,
artists made their homes here, at least for part of the year, as an
alternative to London. The general level of architecture is far finer
than London's. From the local stone, of a yellow-fawn color, sweeping crescents, grand squares, and little alleys were made, all with a
delicacy of design which is seldom found in large and deliberate
projects. And yet Bath was a deliberate project. Orchestrated by a
genius of organization and elegance, "Beau" Nash, social customs
and town streets were painstakingly created. The supposed healing
qualities of the local water were used to draw wealthy visitors. In
the early 1800s, and especially with the coming of the railway, the
town lost some of its cachet; it became too easy for ordinary people

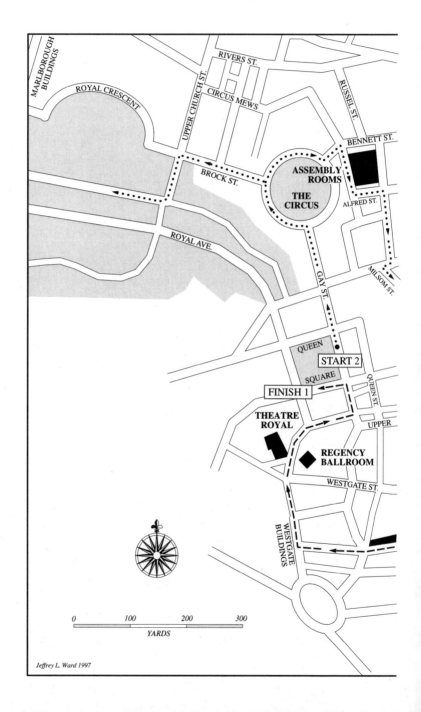

MARLBOROUGH BUILDINGS

RIVERS ST.

ROYAL CRESCENT

UPPER CHURCH ST.

CIRCUS MEWS

RUSSEL ST.

BENNETT ST.

BROCK ST.

ASSEMBLY ROOMS

THE CIRCUS

ALFRED ST.

ROYAL AVE.

GAY ST.

MILSOM ST.

QUEEN

START 2

SQUARE

FINISH 1

QUEEN ST.

THEATRE ROYAL

UPPER

REGENCY BALLROOM

WESTGATE ST.

WESTGATE BUILDINGS

0   100   200   300

YARDS

Jeffrey L. Ward 1997

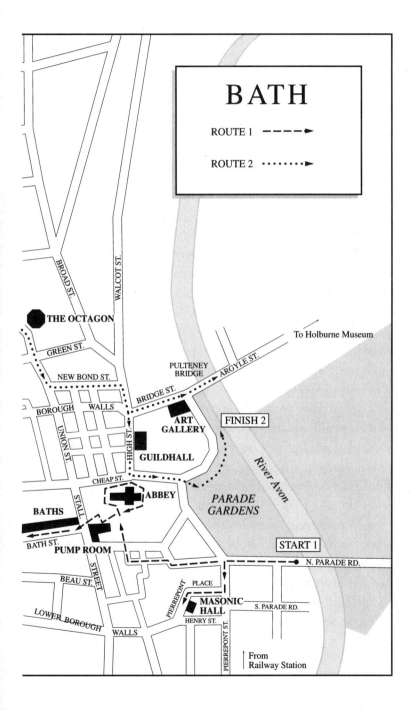

to reach. But heavy industry and arterial roads never came. This is still a town which belongs to the walker. Bath is easily reached by train from London (Paddington station) in about ninety minutes.

There is so much to see in Bath that two walks are suggested so that each can be completed in a morning or an afternoon.

Start your first walk at **North Parade Bridge** over the **River Avon.** Standing here you have a picturesque view along the river of **Pulteney Bridge,** the Italian-style bridge designed by Robert Adam and the **public gardens** just below on your left. Often you will see swans swimming in the stream.

Look all around you and into the distance, to enjoy Bath's setting amid gentle hills and to see the effect of the warm local stone. In front of Pulteney Bridge is a weir. Far behind it, grand terraces of houses stretch across hillsides. And on the skyline to your left is the **Abbey.**

From the bridge walk one hundred yards west (toward the Abbey), along North Parade Road. On the way look for commemorative metal plaques on the houses. At No. 11 lived Edmund Burke, a political theorist who sought to disprove the republican and wealth-sharing ideas of Tom Paine and the French revolutionaries. In one memorable phrase he urged the rich to organize in defense of their wealth against the "combinations" of the radicals: "Where the bad combine, the good must *associate.*" That last word captures nicely the languid understatement fashionable among aristocrats of the day. Fervor and overstatement were dreadfully vulgar. Three houses farther on lived the romantic poet William Wordsworth, for whom the great horror was not political revolution but industrial revolution. Here, far from grimy factories, he had the river and its swans.

At the corner of **Pierrepont Street** turn left and pause at No. 2 where Lord Nelson stayed while visiting Bath. Nelson became for the British, especially their rulers, a hero on a scale hard to imagine today. His leadership warded off the navy of France, and thus kept away the terrors of the French revolution. Across the street go through the pillars into **Pierrepont Place.** At No. 1 worked—as a nursemaid—the young Emma, the future Lady Hamilton. She became the mistress of Lord Nelson and the statuesque icon of her age. After Nelson's death, at the moment of his greatest triumph against the French, even his glorious memory could not save Emma from disapproval, as a parvenue and loose woman. In debt, she fled her creditors and died poor—in France.

Walk along Pierrepont Place and around the corner to the left a few yards to the old **Bath Theatre** (now a Masonic hall) on **Old Orchard Street.** Here Mrs. Sarah Siddons gave her famous performances of Sheridan's *School for Scandal* and *The Rivals.*

Returning to Pierrepont Street, turn left on the wide sidewalk of North Parade and wander down narrow **Lilliput Alley** past some of the city's oldest houses. The alley leads into a quaint square, known as **Abbey Green.** A huge plane tree shades the delightful green, which is close to several antique shops. You will discover as you stroll about the city that Bath is a great antiques center, one of the most noted in the country. From Abbey Green stroll up **Church Street** (to the right of Lilliput Lane) to **Bath Abbey.**

An exquisite gem of Bath stone, the Abbey is a cruciform church in Perpendicular style. Although the present building dates from 1499, a Christian church has stood here for over twelve hundred years. A Norman church, of which only a few bits remain, was destroyed by fire before the erection of the Abbey.

Stroll around to the right of the Abbey to the little square opposite the great **east window** so you can admire the beautiful stonework, the flying buttresses, and the pinnacled tower. On your way round to the **west entrance** of the Abbey, notice the little Victorian statue of a chaste-looking woman carrying water. "Water is best" says its legend. You immediately guess what the sponsors of the statue really meant. Behind is the name of the local Temperance Association.

Before you go in the west entrance, stop for a moment to notice the remarkable carving on the west front—a representation of the founder's dream of saints and angels ascending and descending a ladder from heaven. There are ladders both left and right of the great **Perpendicular window.** Notice the long, medieval skirts of the climbing figures and the one falling angel on the left.

On entering the Abbey you will be struck by the magnificence of the roof **fan vaulting.** The great number of huge windows flood the Abbey with a brightness most unusual in English cathedrals. Though rather small in size, the Abbey has a grace and lovely atmosphere that is quite unmatched. Wander down the nave to the choir to see the new east window, which replaced one bombed out during World War II. Don't miss the fine wrought iron **grille** in the north transept, the superb **fan vaulting** in the north aisle, or the richly carved **chantry of Prior Birde** on the south side of the sanctuary. If you are lucky, you may hear the excellent organ.

On leaving the west door, you will be in the Abbey **churchyard,** a large court. To your left is the entrance to the great **baths,** probably the oldest health establishment in the world (in summer open Monday–Saturday, 9:00–6:00; in winter, Monday–Saturday, 9:00–5:00; Sunday, 10:00–5:00).

Before touring the Roman baths, visit the **Pump Room,** a stately eighteenth-century assembly room, now a café. As you enter, look sharp left. There is a statue of Beau Nash, and below it a long-case clock given in 1709 by Thomas Tompion, perhaps the most famous clockmaker ever. Beside the clock are two sedan chairs, in which ladies and invalids of the 1700s were carried by sweating men. You will admire the exquisite crystal chandelier.

You should now descend to the **Roman baths** where the water gushes forth at the rate of half a million gallons a day at one hundred twenty degrees Fahrenheit. A channel at one end of the bath allows you to dip your fingers to feel the heat of the water. It is worthwhile taking a guided tour.

The remarkably preserved Great Roman Bath, open to the sky, is the center of the establishment which the Romans used for three hundred and fifty years. The six-foot-deep pool is eighty feet long and forty feet wide. The huge blocks of Bath stone around the pool and the diving stone date from the Roman period, as does much of the pool's lead lining. Parts of the lead conduit were laid by Roman plumbers almost two thousand years ago. There is an unusual view of Bath Abbey's tower from here. While touring the baths, notice the Roman system of underfloor heating. In a small antechamber you can see the source of the hot spring water.

You will see a model of the Roman remains and also wonderful Roman relics. Two of the finest pieces are the pediment of the Sulis Minerva Temple and the beautiful gilded bronze head of the goddess. Other fascinating relics are the Roman memorial stones and a Roman curse engraved on lead, expressing a young man's frustration over losing a woman's favors.

Go round to the side of the Pump Room furthest from the Abbey, and look for **Bath Street.** Stroll along Bath Street, one of the few streets in England colonnaded on both sides. At the foot of the street stands the medieval **Cross Bath** where Mary of Modena, James II's Queen, bathed. A cross which formerly stood here celebrated the birth of a son to Mary in 1688, after bathing in these healthy waters. This baby brought disaster to his parents. As a boy he stood to inherit the throne before his Protestant half-sisters, but he would be brought up as a Catholic, like both his parents. The fear of an indefinite Catholic succession caused the mainly Protestant ruling class to eject James II and his family. James's Protestant daughter Mary and her husband William of Orange were installed instead. (Bath's Tourist Information office is now twenty yards away.)

Turn right at the Cross Bath and left into the passage that runs beside the Little Theatre. On reaching a road, turn right and see two hundred yards away the Theatre Royal. Walk to it. The **Popjoys Restaurant,** just beyond the theater, used to be the home of Bath's uncrowned king, Beau Nash, where he died in 1761. As you stand with your left shoulder to the Theatre, opposite and to your right is the street called **Upper Borough Walls.** Go into it, then turn first left into **Trim Street.** Before you reach the arch, called **Trim Bridge,** you will notice at No. 5 a large house with a decorative doorway on the right. General Wolfe, the hero of the Battle of Quebec during the French and Indian Wars, lived here in the mid-eighteenth century. Carved in stone above the door are symbols of soldiering and power: musket, helmet, quiver, arrows, and (the Roman symbols of authority) rods and ax.

Beyond the arch you will be in picturesque, cobbled **Queen Street** with many small, quaint houses and little shops. This is one of the most attractive corners of Bath where you may want to wander about and browse.

At the top of Queen Street turn right into **Quiet Street.** An excellent antique shop specializing in furniture is on your right.

Retrace your steps on Quiet Street and cross over to Wood Street. This will lead you to **Queen Square,** one of the most charming in the city. The classic and beautifully proportioned **north façade** designed by John Wood Senior is an excellent example of his distinguished architecture. His home was No. 24. In front of the door is the frame of an eighteenth-century oil lamp. While you are strolling around the square, which encircles a pleasant little park, it is interesting to recall that the novelist Jane Austen, who lived in

Bath at various times during her life, resided at No. 13 in 1798. Above and to the left of the fanlight is the metal badge of a private eighteenth-century fire brigade—the Sun company. The badge shows father sun and his rays. Without a badge such as this, a private brigade would not tackle your fire. Two of Jane Austen's novels, *Persuasion* and *Northanger Abbey,* are connected with Bath and describe vividly life in Bath at the beginning of the nineteenth century. The latter novel contains delicate satire of the social round at Bath. Austen describes a young lady of quality who complains to her friend about two quite dreadful young gentlemen who are following them, while considerately stopping from time to time to ensure that the two young men do not lose sight of them in the crowd. This charming square, with its literary associations, is a good place to end this first walk through Bath.

❧ Bath II

This second walk through Bath will show you some of the best eighteenth-century taste in civic planning.

At the northeast corner of Queen Square cross over to **No. 41 Gay Street** on the corner of **Old King Street.** This was the home of John Wood the Younger who carried on the magnificent classical building of his father. From the street, to the right of the door, you can see the small powder room. In its decorative recess the gentlemen and ladies of the period used to powder their wigs.

Continue along Gay Street past stone houses to **George Street,** the next on your right. Take a left turn into the little pedestrian street called **Miles's Buildings.** Even in this unpretentious setting there are stylish housefronts. Look at the wrought iron balcony at No. 6. Come back to the corner with George Street and go left for a moment—or for several hours!—to the Hole-in-the-Wall restaurant, very highly recommended for cooking in the French style. As in many elegant restaurants in Britain, prices are lower at lunchtime.

Go back to Gay Street and walk a few yards uphill to **the Circus.** The uniform beauty of this superb group of four-story houses that encircles the central green shaded by five plane trees is quite exceptional. Designed by John Wood the Elder and begun in 1754, these fine Palladian-style homes, with extensive gardens at the back, have recently been refaced. The Circus was so laid out that there is a true crescent between each of the three streets which lead off from it. Note the crowning acorns and the frieze that runs along the top of the entire circular group. Many distinguished people lived in the Circus. At No. 14 lived Lord Clive, who, without any formal military training, founded the British empire in India by outgeneralling the French; Major André (of the American Revolutionary War) lived at No. 22, and Thomas Gainsborough at No. 17.

Bear left into **Brock Street;** look at the lovely stone doorway of No. 16, and the "light" above it (the arrangement of metal in the glass). At the end turn left into one of Bath's lovely parks. As you stroll along, you will see the gardens of the houses you have just passed and the beautifully planted flower beds in the park.

Look right to the magnificent sweep of **Royal Crescent,** often called "the finest crescent in Europe." The sheer expanse of this dramatic architectural masterpiece is in itself overwhelming. Built between 1767 and 1775, these thirty houses constitute a noble ellipse over six hundred feet long. One hundred and fourteen tall Ionic columns support one continuous cornice designed in the monumental Palladian style. Pause for a while to absorb this stupendous architectural effect.

Returning to **Brock Street** (unless you want to have a close look at the houses in Royal Crescent), turn left in a few yards along a passageway called **Margaret's Buildings** lined with small shops.

Now go back to the Circus, bear left on **Bennett Street** and take a sharp right to the **Bath Assembly Rooms.** This is another architectural triumph of John Wood the Younger. Bombed out during World War II, the beautiful ballroom, with its lovely high plaster ceiling, has now been restored to its original splendor. The five exquisite chandeliers are pre-Waterford glass and were made in London about 1771 (open weekdays, 10:00–5:00; Sundays, 11:00–5:00). Be sure to visit downstairs the intensely interesting **Museum of Costume.** Its collection includes fashionable men's and women's clothing from the days of Beau Nash to the present. Many of the costumes are shown against a background of Bath. The earliest complete dress, and the pride of the collection, is the **Silver Tissue Dress** from around 1660, made of cream silk and metal thread. The dress has an air of alluring simplicity, expensively achieved. It would have suited well an age in which puritan tastes were being overtaken by royalist luxury. (In 1660 Britain's brief republic ended, and Charles II was brought to the throne.) From three hundred years later, the museum also has striking dresses by Mary Quant and her contemporaries. And from the heyday of Bath there are costumes of dandies and grand dames from the 1700s.

Turn left from the Assembly Rooms into **Alfred Street.** No. 14 (**Alfred House**) has a pair of iron torch snuffers on either side of the front door. Note also the cogs of a former pulley on the left of the door which was added in the days of Queen Victoria for the purpose of raising beer barrels at the time the house was occupied by resident employees of an adjoining department store.

From Alfred Street go first right into **Bartlett Street** where you will find several antique shops. At the bottom turn right, then first left, and stroll along **Milsom Street,** Bath's distinguished shopping street. One hundred yards along Milsom Street, on the left, explore Shires Yard, now an interestingly designed modern precinct of small shops, and formerly, around 1770, a stableyard from which horses went clattering out with carriages to London, carrying portraits of grandees by Thomas Gainsborough.

At the end of Milsom Street cross over into **Old Bond Street,** about fifty yards long and only for pedestrians. From it you will see the imposing Georgian façade of the **Royal Mineral Water Hospital,** its name picked out in great gold letters. After browsing a bit in the attractive old shops here, turn into **New Bond Street.** D. and B. Dickinson on the left is well known for silverware.

From the end of New Bond Street cross toward The Podium shopping mall, then look left. One hundred yards away is the **Saracen's Head,** Bath's most ancient pub where Charles Dickens stayed while preparing *Pickwick Papers.* The interior is dark and intimate.

From the Saracen's Head go back past the end of New Bond Street toward the Abbey. Go left at Bridge Street and in a few moments you will be at the eighteenth-century **Pulteney Bridge,** one of Europe's few bridges (like Florence's Ponte Vecchio) that is lined with shops. You can see right through some of the shops, to the river beyond. At the end of the bridge, on the right, go down the steps for a dramatic view of the riverside colonnade opposite. (You will reach the colonnade itself in a few minutes.) Come back up the steps and cross the bridge once more.

From Pulteney Bridge return along Bridge Street and go left on **High Street.** Here on your left are **Bath City Markets,** a lively spot where, under arcades, you will find stalls selling books, bric-a-brac, cheese. Look for the short eighteenth-century pillar on which deals were done and cash laid down. Go into the **Guildhall** right next door on High Street. The upstairs **Banqueting Room,** elaborately decorated in the Adam style with a beautiful stucco ceiling, ornamental frieze, and eighteenth-century pre-Waterford glass chandeliers, is a magnificent hall (open Monday–Friday). Look up to the delicate cast iron of the minstrels' gallery and to the oval Georgian windows.

Turn left from the Guildhall, cross over behind the Abbey, and go into the **Parade Gardens** on the riverside. Walk to the river's edge, in the direction of Pulteney Bridge, and you will be in the colonnade, its sections slightly angled so that your path between the columns seems to stretch away forever. With the weir below you and the elegant bridge ahead, this is a lovely spot to end the walk.

Cambridge I ❧

Compared with Oxford, **Cambridge** has the more obvious beauty. The *courts* of Cambridge colleges seem more spacious than the quads of Oxford. And the colleges lie more compactly together. There is one central band, along the River Cam, where seven colleges abut the river, each with a riverside garden. This stretch, where the famous punts glide (or helplessly zigzag!) amid elegant bridges, is known as the **Backs.** And the most notable section of the Backs belongs to **King's College,** whose late medieval chapel—in effect, a lofty cathedral—can be seen for many miles across the flat, formerly Fenland, countryside.

Cambridge was founded in the Middle Ages by dissidents from Oxford. There is still a marked difference in atmosphere between the two universities. Oxford is the more relaxed, with humor more in evidence. Cambridge has a greater proportion of scientists, and its humanities students have, over centuries, followed continental fashions with intensity. During the Reformation, Cambridge was called "little Germany" because of its respect for Luther's new

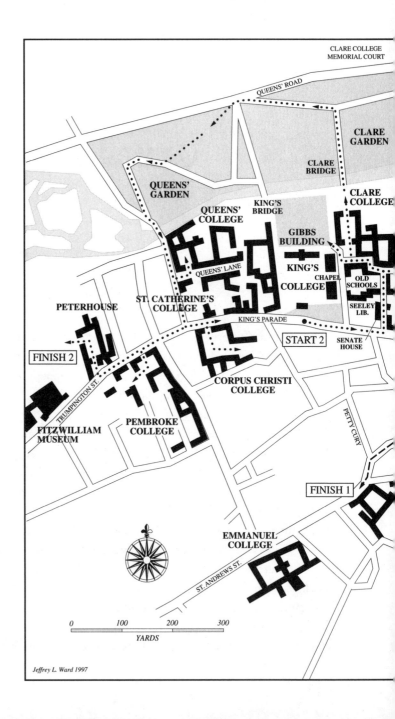

CLARE COLLEGE
MEMORIAL COURT

QUEENS' ROAD

CLARE
GARDEN

CLARE
BRIDGE

QUEENS'
GARDEN

CLARE
COLLEGE

QUEENS'
COLLEGE

KING'S
BRIDGE

GIBBS
BUILDING

QUEENS' LANE

KING'S
COLLEGE

CHAPEL

OLD
SCHOOLS

ST. CATHERINE'S
COLLEGE

SEELEY
LIB.

PETERHOUSE

KING'S PARADE

START 2

SENATE
HOUSE

FINISH 2

CORPUS CHRISTI
COLLEGE

PETTY CURY

TRUMPINGTON ST.

PEMBROKE
COLLEGE

FITZWILLIAM
MUSEUM

FINISH 1

EMMANUEL
COLLEGE

ST. ANDREWS ST.

0   100   200   300
YARDS

Jeffrey L. Ward 1997

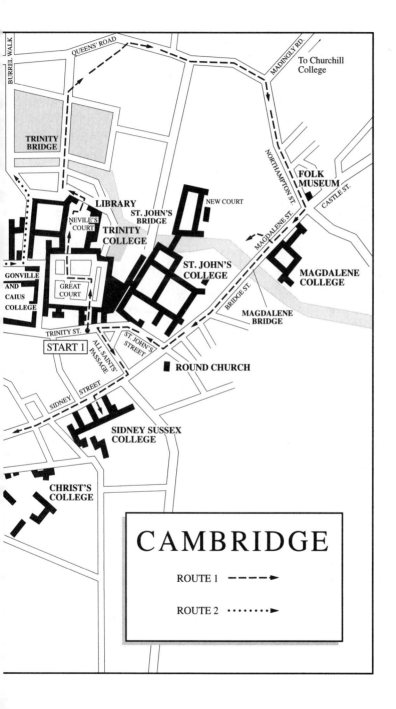

BURREL WALK

QUEENS' ROAD

MADINGLY RD.

To Churchill College

TRINITY BRIDGE

NORTHAMPTON ST.

FOLK MUSEUM

CASTLE ST.

LIBRARY

NEW COURT

ST. JOHN'S BRIDGE

NEVILE'S COURT

TRINITY COLLEGE

MAGDALENE ST.

ST. JOHN'S COLLEGE

MAGDALENE COLLEGE

GONVILLE AND CAIUS COLLEGE

GREAT COURT

BRIDGE ST.

MAGDALENE BRIDGE

TRINITY ST.

START 1

ALL SAINT'S PASSAGE

ST. JOHN'S STREET

ROUND CHURCH

SIDNEY   STREET

SIDNEY SUSSEX COLLEGE

CHRIST'S COLLEGE

CAMBRIDGE

ROUTE 1 ----->

ROUTE 2 ·······>

protestantism. In the 1640s Cambridge was at the heart of the puritanism from which Parliament and Cromwell drew their armies; their opponents, King Charles I and his high church supporters, had their headquarters in Oxford. In the 1930s Oxford students scandalously announced that they would not fight obediently for "King and Country." At Cambridge things were less showy, but more intense. Here, an important group of intellectuals quietly got on with spying for the Soviet Union. During the student power era, around 1970, it was Cambridge students who were given long terms of imprisonment for conspiracy to riot. And in the 1990s the Parisian intellectual fashion of Deconstructive Theory penetrated Cambridge, while at Oxford it was viewed more coolly.

The town of Cambridge is smaller than Oxford, and its traffic less intrusive. The main streets through the university area have recently been barred to most vehicles. It is now more peaceful to walk along **Trinity Street** and **King's Parade** than it has been for a century. In choosing which to visit first, Cambridge or Oxford, consider the weather. On a cool day, elegant Cambridge can be chill; Cambridge people say that the east wind reaches them uninterrupted from western Russia. Oxford, with its smaller quads, is more sheltered, more intimate. But on a warm day, especially in spring, the riverside walks of Cambridge are incomparable.

Cambridge is reached by rail from London's King's Cross station; the train takes about an hour. From the Cambridge railway station there are frequent buses to the center of town. The most popular of the colleges now charge visitors for admission. At exam times (April–May) they may be closed. If you plan to visit then, it may be well to check first with Cambridge's Tourist Information office. Its number is given below.

Begin your walk through Cambridge at the largest college of all, **Trinity.** Pause for a few minutes on **Trinity Street** before the

court, close to the lawn, are the forgotten brackets of eighteenth-century oil lamps. Wren created one of his masterpieces in his design of the **library** whose noble façade of slightly pink stone rises above the loggia.

At the far right-hand corner, in the cloister, you go up a flight of steps to the library (open weekdays 2:15–4:45; Saturday, 10:45–12:45). Its interior, beautifully proportioned, "touches the very soul of anyone who first sees it," Roger North wrote in 1695 after its completion. Wren even designed the tall bookcases as well as tables and chairs in the alcoves. Grinling Gibbons's carvings are superb examples of his best work. At the far end of the library you can see part of Newton's private book collection and diaries. The library's treasures include John Milton's handwritten manuscripts of his shorter poems, and many rare illuminated manuscripts.

From the library go through a gate to the river, then walk eighty yards to the left and cross **Trinity Bridge** to **the Avenue**—one of the best known walks in Cambridge. From the bridge you have a memorable vista in either direction—St. John's on your right and the chimneys of Trinity Hall (a separate college) on the left. Pause for a moment on the other side of the bridge and look back at the stately library with the river and green lawn in the foreground. Looking in the opposite direction from the Wren Library, the modern tower you may see in the distance, through trees, belongs to the **University Library** ("The U.L.," to Cambridge students, many of whom are in awe of the place, because of its crowds of intense readers.) Stark outside, intimidating inside, the U.L.'s tower is sometimes compared to the chimney of a crematorium.

Turn right on the footpath beside the willows that shade the river. In a moment you will have a grand view of the tower of **St. John's Chapel.** Shortly you are faced by an iron bridge into **St. John's garden.** The gate is now shut; the colleges close their borders to help with the collection of admission fees. Go back to Trinity Bridge;

don't cross it—turn right, walk the length of the Avenue, go through elaborate iron gates and cross the water-filled ditch, one of a series which still protects the Backs of the colleges. Take the path which goes about forty-five degrees right from Trinity gate and which reaches the sidewalk of Queens' Road. Walk several hundred yards along the right-hand side of Queens' Road, passing on the right the high formal gates of St. John's College and then a pleasant villa, behind yew trees, dating from around 1900. Keep right at the first road junction. Thirty yards past it, go right for a moment to view a small, quiet courtyard of cottages with steep, shouldered roofs.

Return to the road, **Northampton Street,** and continue to the right. Opposite is a pub called the "**Town and Gown.**" This is a common and important phrase in Cambridge life. "Gown" is shorthand for university people, because until the 1960s they commonly wore academic gowns in the streets, and students were required to wear gowns in public after dark. (The fine for disobedience was six shillings and eight pence—half of a mark, a medieval unit of currency.) "Town" means the non-university majority. There were, and still remain, tensions between Town and Gown. Town people used to argue that the university excluded industry from Cambridge and thus, deliberately or not, kept down wages. Town lads earned a pittance serving meals to their privileged contemporaries in college halls. Many an undergraduate got a bowl of hot soup spilt "accidentally" down the back of his neck by the town boy waiting on him. There would then be a great fuss, as the soup was mopped from "Sir's" gown. Town women of mature years were employed by the colleges as "bedders." Nominally they were to keep young men's rooms from descending into squalor. More seriously they were meant to report to the college authorities if a young man was sleeping with a woman in his rooms. The students got round this by doing their "sleeping" in the daytime. Ladies went away in the evening. (The last train from Cambridge to London on Sunday evenings, at 9:10, was known as "The Whores' Express.") This world of pseudomonasticism policed by college servants largely passed away in the 1970s. The colleges are now coed.

Northampton Street widens as you approach a busy junction. On the right, cottages have two upper stories which each "jetty out" beyond the story below. On the corner of **Castle Street** (to your left) is the **Cambridge Folk Museum** (open Tuesday–Saturday, 10:30–5:00; Sunday, 2:00–5:00). It consists of exhibits depicting the trades, occupations, and domestic crafts illustrating the life and work of Cambridge people from medieval times. There are also several children's rooms and exhibits of rural life.

Turn right into **Magdalene Street** (pronounced Maudlin). In a few yards on your right you pass a row of old houses with projecting stories, bay windows, and russet-tiled steep hipped roofs. In a moment you will cross the road to pass through the main entrance of **Magdalene College.** But first turn right into a little-known and delightful courtyard, **Benson Court,** also belonging to Magdalene. Here, on the right, is a superb half-timbered building. Just beyond it, high up on a wall, are a **pair of modern sundials,** one calibrated for the months January through June, the other for July through December. An inscription in Latin refers with grimly erudite Cambridge humor to the discrepancies between sundials: *Facilius inter philosophos quam inter horologia conveniet.* ("[Even] philosophers will agree sooner than sundials.")

Go a few yards farther along the path, then turn left to reach the river. Here, between high, echoing walls, punts tangle entertainingly on a narrow stretch of water. There is a fine weeping willow to sit by, as you enjoy the architecture of St. John's College opposite. Away to your right, look for the **Bridge of Sighs,** also part of "John's." This intimate spot by the willow is one of the hidden delights of Cambridge. Many pass it on the river, but few know how to reach it, since Magdalene is not a favorite with visitors. Should you be thinking of refreshment, the **Pickerel pub** is only a few yards away, just this side of Magdalene Bridge. (You will pass it in a moment; the bridge you can already see on your left.)

Go back to Magdalene Street. Go a few yards to the right, then cross to enter the main court of the college. The old red brickwork has recently been cleaned and the crests have been repainted, giving the buildings a fresh appearance. There is a charming, intimate feeling about this court, part of which on your right was once a fifteenth-century Benedictine abbey. Continue to the second court to visit the famous **Pepys Library** (open 2:30–3:30 in term). It is above the arcade of the lovely English Renaissance building. Pepys's fascinating books are kept in the original oak shelves he had made for them. His collection also includes the manuscript volumes of his diary, a documentation of political and sexual scandal from the 1660s which (in the modern, uncensored edition by Latham and Matthews) makes delightful bedside reading. Look in the index for references to "Deb Willett," Pepys's young servant and mistress, and to his employer Charles II ("The king does spend all his time with his mistresses, kissing and feeling them naked. But this lechery will never leave him."). Stroll around the charming **garden** to the left of the Pepys building. Its informality and beautiful flowers, especially its exquisite roses, make it one of the most delightful in Cambridge.

Returning to Magdalene Street, you turn left to cross **Magdalene Bridge** over **the Cam,** the shallowest point where the river could be forded. This is the place from which Cambridge gets its name. Here in the mid-1960s an intense local event took place, fun, but with overtones once more of the grim Cambridge humor and puritanism. On a winter night of celebration, the life-size effigy of a woman undergraduate, a Ms. Suzy Menkes, was carried in triumph to the bridge. Ms. Menkes was at the time a journalist with the student newspaper and had got herself noted by seeming to hint in her column ("Annabel's Diary") at a string of social successes with male undergraduates who were gorgeous, intriguing, and rich. The ratio of men to women in the university was about nine to one. Most of these men were not gorgeous, intriguing, or rich. And many of them had no sexual successes at all. On learning that "Annabel" was to get her comeuppance on Magdalene Bridge, a great crowd of students gathered. A deep cheer of male togetherness went up as "Annabel" was lit and, trailing flames, was pitched from the bridge into the muddy waters of the Cam. (Menkes had the last laugh. She quickly became a leading fashion correspondent for a national newspaper.)

Two hundred yards farther on your left you will come to the **Round Church,** landscaped by a little rose garden. The oldest of only four round churches in England, it dates from the crusaders (1130) and was planned after the Church of the Holy Sepulcher in Jerusalem. Around its door is the dog-tooth design favored by early Norman architects. The interior, much restored, has massive pillars and a delightful gallery with rounded, romanesque, arches.

On leaving the church, retrace your steps to the right for a few yards, then cross the road to head for **St. John's College,** with its massive **Victorian chapel tower.** Its imposing gate tower in dark red brick and stone is emblazoned with the brilliantly painted and gilded Tudor rose, and the shield of the founder, Lady Margaret Beaufort, mother of Henry VII.

The recent cleaning of St. John's second court adds to the beauty of the fine Elizabethan brickwork. During the renovation the **Tudor Tower** at the far side of the court was largely rebuilt with the original bricks. Proceed through the third court to the **Bridge of Sighs.**

Go back to the gatehouse and go down a narrow passageway opposite the gatehouse, next to a tiny churchyard and turn left in **All Saints' Passage.** The area on the left was Cambridge's ancient Jewry. On reaching **Bridge Street** cross over, turn right, and shortly you will come to **Sidney Sussex College.** This was Oliver

Cromwell's college. His skull is buried near the entrance to the chapel. It was separated from his body by no accident. Cromwell had taken the lead in arranging the execution of Charles I. In 1660, with Cromwell dead, royal power returned. To gain posthumous revenge, royalists dug up Cromwell's corpse and mounted its head on the roof of Westminster Hall, where Charles I had been tried and sentenced to death. This was concrete propaganda, to demonstrate—at the seat of Cromwell's formal power—which side had really won.

Continue along busy Sidney Street, usually crowded with shoppers, for a few hundred yards to **Christ's College** on your left. Before you enter, look at the early **Tudor gateway.** It is similar in elaborate decoration to St. John's, with the same Beaufort "Yales," for both were founded by Lady Margaret Beaufort. **John Milton** is the college's most distinguished old member. **Darwin's** room was to the right of the gatehouse. The garden, one of Cambridge's loveliest, is outstanding for the variety of its trees and shrubs as well as for its herbaceous borders. This is a good spot to end the walk. Beyond Christ's College the animation and atmosphere of the medieval town center fade away.

CAMBRIDGE II ⚜

Start this walk through the enchanting courts and scenic Backs of the colleges at **King's Parade,** on the cobbles outside **King's College.** The porter's **lodge,** with many pinnacles, is set in a gothic stone screen. You will probably need to enter the college by a different route, but look for a moment through the entrance here. Beyond the great lawn is the rather chilly eighteenth-century splendor of the Gibbs Building, where many of King's teachers have rooms. (The academic staff of Cambridge and Oxford colleges are known as "Fellows," or "Senior Members"; less formally as "dons.") On the near side of the lawn you will see a small metal sign: "Please keep off the grass unless accompanied by a senior member of the college." At Cambridge, to walk on a college lawn is a badge of status, jealously guarded. Sometimes a don can be seen making a special detour in order to do it. Soaring above you to the right is Cambridge's most famous building, **King's College Chapel.** We shall need a detour of our own to reach it.

Walk along King's Parade, passing the back of King's Chapel and the superb chestnut tree next to it. You reach a corner on the left where, behind massive spiked railings of the eighteenth century, stands the university's **Senate House.** Here, degrees are handed out in a ceremony each June. More importantly, notice boards outside the building announce publicly who in examinations has triumphed ("Got a First"), or got the dreaded norm, a Lower Second (a "Two-Two"). At the end of May, young people can be seen reeling away from the notice boards, aghast or elated. At Cambridge, there is thought to be a certain chivalry about getting the lowest class of honors degree, a Third. The theory is, a Two-Two may represent an indifferent person, who has worked hard but unsuccessfully. The person with a Third, on the other hand, has clearly been doing something else. The ideal of the languid aristocrat is still alive here. At Oxford there was until recently a Fourth Class, for those who had really been doing nothing. This was known as "a Gentleman's Degree." If you are in Cambridge in April or May, you may wonder why the students are so little in evidence. The explanation is, they are shut away reviewing ("swotting") for exams. Class of degree, even pass and fail, rests entirely on performance in three sets of exams, spread over three years. Course work does not count. Every spring each student faces an all-or-nothing ordeal.

Turn the corner, left, into **Senate House Passage.** Look up. High above, perhaps fifty feet up, the roof of the Senate House almost reaches a parapet of Caius College (written "Gonville and Caius," pronounced "Keys.") Between the roofs is a gap of perhaps six feet. Here was performed a ritual of young manhood—the "Senate House Leap." Late at night a small group of undergraduates would climb the Senate House then jump across to Caius. To fall, onto the cobbles far below, was almost certain death. As the university in recent decades has become more academic, less sporting in tone, the feat has perhaps died out. In the 1960s a pair of undergraduates were "sent down" (expelled) from the university for, in the deliberately dry official phrase, "climbing on the Senate House." Their names, still remembered with awe and sympathy, were Rollin and McConville.

About halfway down Senate House Passage, on the left, a gate opens to a modern building with "Bibliotheca" ("library") at the entrance. Above the door of this, the University's law library, are some traces of graffiti which even the unrelenting authorities of Cambridge might not wish to see removed. There are five "V"s and two sets of the Morse Code signs for "V": • • • —. These almost certainly date from the celebrations at the end of World War II. "V" (for Victory) had been Churchill's slogan to occupied Europe. The rhythm of • • • — was conveyed by the BBC with the opening four notes of Beethoven's Fifth Symphony.

On returning to Senate House Passage, you are facing the Renaissance **Gate of Honour** of **Gonville and Caius College.** Blue and gold sundials decorate the cupola. Go through this gate into the simple court with a charming clock tower on the far side. This is **Caius Court,** exceptional among the brick and faded stone of Cambridge for the warmth of its yellow stone and for the intimacy of its scale. The roofs of the buildings are steep. So are the stairs within. There is a story among Caius people that a philosophy don who lived recently in this court, an intense and deeply religious character, used to rejoin the world each morning by levitating down the stairs. On the right is the **Gate of Virtue** which, according to the plan of the college's benefactor, Dr. Caius, the student traversed after entering the **Gate of Humility** on Trinity Street and before leaving the Gate of Honor to get his degree in the Senate House. Dr. Caius in the sixteenth century named his gates in Latin: *Humilitatis, Virtutis, Honoris.* Undergraduates of Caius in the last few years have identified a symbolic gate of their own. A low archway on the far side of the college leads to an austere set of toilets. In chalk above the archway a hand has written *Necessitatis*—the Gate of Necessity.

Walk to the far end of Senate House Passage. Turn right and then first left into the gaunt passage called **Garret Hostel Lane.** One hundred fifty yards along here you will reach a graceful modern **bridge,** and a view of the Backs. A few yards before the bridge, a plaque set in the wall of Trinity Hall, on your left, says of the bridge, "It was designed by Timothy Guy Morgan, an undergraduate of Jesus College, who died in that year [1960]." Notice how the gently curving bridge harmonizes with the trees along the river banks. Look upriver for the view: first Trinity Hall with its great Copper Beech tree, then Clare College with its stone bridge (which you may cross in a few minutes), and in the distance King's College and King's bridge. Notice, too, the roofscapes and the chimneys, Cambridge's specialty.

Retrace your route up Garret Hostel Lane. Turn right and follow **Trinity Lane** past the entrance to Senate House Passage until you reach the railings which mark the boundary of King's College, where there is an entrance fee to pay. A few yards ahead, and already towering above you, is King's College Chapel.

Enter the chapel, often called the noblest Gothic monument and finest example of Perpendicular style in England. Commenced by Henry VI in 1446, the chapel was completed in 1515.

After stepping inside, you will at once feel humbled by the magnificently proportioned interior. As you glance down the great nave, the beauty of the lofty lacelike **fan vaulting** in stone is extraordinary. The great **rood screen,** considered one of the finest pieces of woodwork in northern Europe, is surmounted by the organ with its four graceful angels. Inquire when the next service will be held and return, if possible, to hear the world-renowned **King's College Choir** in this incomparable setting.

The huge **windows** are the largest and most complete series of antique windows in the world. You should obtain the booklet that describes them in detail. Made between 1515 and 1531 by both

Flemings in England and Englishmen, they represent the best example of Flemish Renaissance **glass painting.** To appreciate their beautiful detail, you should study one or two single figures.

You will want to wander about the various **chantry chapels** and also examine the excellent woodwork of the **choir stalls** and the painting by Rubens of the Adoration of the Magi before you have a last look at this inspiring chapel. On leaving the chapel, look over the great lawn which sweeps down to the river. Leave King's by the same gate. After a few feet, turn left into **Clare College.** Stroll through the college court on your way to Clare Bridge. Just before you reach the river you will pass lovely gardens on either side of the path. Pause for a few moments on **Clare Bridge,** the oldest in Cambridge (1640), with its row of stone balls, for another glance up and down the Cam. This is one of the most idyllic scenes in Cambridge—the punts and boats gliding along the still waters of the Cam under the luxuriant trees, the close-cropped grass banks bordering the narrow stream, and the superb gardens. Just to your right on the far side of the bridge through handsome eighteenth-century iron grill gates resplendent with Clare's crest is probably the most beautiful **garden** of all.

A few yards along the path will bring you to its entrance down a few stone steps. To stroll through this exquisitely laid-out and maintained garden is one of the most delightful experiences in all of Cambridge. The gardens and courtyards of Cambridge are used each summer as sets for Shakespearean plays. Here Clare actors have performed *A Midsummer Night's Dream.* Wander down to the river for a view of Clare Bridge. Circular flower beds, shrubs, and trees are so carefully landscaped that the combination of colors and arrangement of groupings is quite marvelous. Then stroll along the deep herbaceous border, so artistic in gold and blue. This leads to a sunken garden enclosed by a yew hedge—just the spot to sit for a while and revel in this lovely garden.

From Clare Garden saunter down the tree-lined walk to **Queens' Road.** Turn left, passing on your left the famous view of King's Chapel, the Gibbs Building, and the Cam. After passing the gate to King's go left across the Common to **Silver Street.** Look over both sides of Silver Street bridge. On the left is a wooden footbridge between sections of Queens' College, the popularly named "**Mathematical Bridge**" (alleged to be so-called because of the careful calculation of strains in its construction). From the opposite side of Silver Street bridge is a lovely view over a former millpool. A little weir marks the point at which the Cam is deemed to end and its upper section, called the Granta, begins. The bridge over the weir is a favorite place for a pint of beer, brought from the **Mill pub** a few yards away. Down the steps by the **Anchor pub, punts** are hired by the hour. (For advice on the technique of punting see p. 106.) You may be advised here to punt "Cambridge end"—that is, standing on the platform at one end of the craft, rather than in the well of the boat at the other end. Ignore such advice. "Oxford end" is safer; if your foot slips, it is restrained by the side of the boat rather than slipping into the water. You can expect to learn the main techniques of navigation within a few hundred yards—and your hour will be time enough to pass all the famous Backs, and to return to this spot.

Go farther along Silver Street, then turn first left into Queens' Lane for the turreted fifteenth-century gateway which is the entrance to Queens' College. Go through the gateway to the second court, **Cloister Court.** The combination of the mellow deep red brick medieval building with its arched windows above the cloister, the fine oriel windows and façade of the half-timbered President's Lodging, and the high brick wall of the Hall, make this court a gem. Pause for a few minutes in these glorious surroundings to admire the way the maroon color of the brick and the sixteenth-century black and white of the President's Lodgings seem to blend, though so different. Cloister Court has an intimate, restful charm that is quite unique in Cambridge. In recent times the space under the President's Lodge was used as a stage, for the production of *Othello*, in a Tudor setting.

A passageway will lead you to the other side of the President's Lodgings and the new **Erasmus building** in honor of the college's most distinguished old member. This modern building is ingeniously designed. By supporting the building on brick arches and stone pillars and eliminating the ground floor, the architect has preserved a relatively uninterrupted view of the gardens, lawns, and the river bank.

Return to Cloister Court and go into **Queens' Hall,** highly colorful with its medieval decoration and sixteenth-century ceiling. On your way through the first court, dating from 1451, note the elaborate **sundial** below the clock high up under the cupola. Here again you will be impressed by the beauty of the brickwork.

On leaving Queen's by the point at which you entered, turn right and then left into Silver Street. One hundred yards will bring you to **Trumpington Street.** Turn left to see the open courtyard of **St. Catherine's College** ("Cat's"), lofty and frowning in seventeenth-century red brick. Then cross Trumpington Street and go back a few yards in the direction of Silver Street, to see **Corpus Christi College** ("Corpus"). In the first court go to the farthest staircase on the left side; a passage here will lead you to one of the treasures of Cambridge, **Old Court.** Completed in 1377, the Old Court is the earliest example of a complete medieval quadrangle still standing. You will be fascinated by its ancient doorways and medieval windows.

Back at Corpus's main gate, turn left into Trumpington Street, and immediately after passing the junction with **Pembroke Street,** on the left, go into **Pembroke College** and look right. You will see the **college chapel,** designed by Christopher Wren. This is the first building he created (1663), his formal training having been as an astronomer. There is a lovely glass lantern on the chapel roof.

Back out in Trumpington Street, turn left and cross the road to enter Peterhouse, founded in 1284 and the oldest college in Cambridge. Just inside the front court you will see the seventeenth-century **chapel** with a classical loggia on either side—an unusual architectural design. The **hall** and **buttery** in the old court behind are substantially as they were in the thirteenth century. Just beyond the Hall go through the small studded door, the next to last on the left, and you can enter Peterhouse's extensive **gardens.** Wander through the gardens to see the new eight-story modern dormitory building, one of the best in Cambridge and sometimes called Peterhouse's skyscraper. Actors at Peterhouse recently used their garden, in the haunted silence of a spring evening, for a production of Euripides's tragedy of wild nature, *The Bacchae.* In the final scene, the god Dionysos appears in vindictive triumph, out of human reach. In the Peterhouse production, Dionysos made his sudden appearance on top of the skyscraper.

You should end this tour of Cambridge by visiting the **Fitzwilliam Museum** (open weekdays, except Mondays, 10:00–5:00; Sunday, 2:15–5:00) just a few yards beyond Peterhouse. The spacious and well-lighted Fitzwilliam galleries contain one of the finest collections of art and antiquities outside London. Although the museum's department of Egyptian, Greek, Roman, and medieval art is outstanding, including notable exhibits of coins, pottery, porcelain, and medieval manuscripts, you may be particularly interested in the paintings and prints. The Italian, Dutch, and English schools are well represented, and the Fitzwilliam also possesses an unusually interesting selection of French impressionists.

Here, in these artistic surroundings, you can try and decide which colleges you want to revisit on your next trip to Cambridge.

Phone: Tourist Information, Cambridge: 01223 322640

CANTERBURY ⚜

Canterbury has been the source and seat of Christianity in England since St. Augustine founded his mission for the Pagan English in 597. The Archbishop of Canterbury (whose main palace is at Lambeth in central London) is head of the Anglican church worldwide. This small Kentish city, at the end of the Pilgrim's Way, calls to mind Thomas Becket, Chaucer's *Canterbury Tales,* the medieval pilgrimages, and in a later period the Elizabethan poet, Christopher Marlowe. But Canterbury's history goes back at least a thousand years before the coming of St. Augustine.

In the Roman period a commercial community, Durovernum, grew up at this ancient ford over the River Stour. Though the name Canterbury comes from the Saxon *cant-wara-burh,* meaning "Stronghold of Men of Kent," Canterbury's appeal to today's visitor, as for the medieval pilgrim is expressed by the city's motto with its religious connotation—"Ave Mater Angliae"—"Hail, Mother of England."

As you stroll around this once walled city, only two hours from London (Charing Cross Station) by rail, you will realize that,

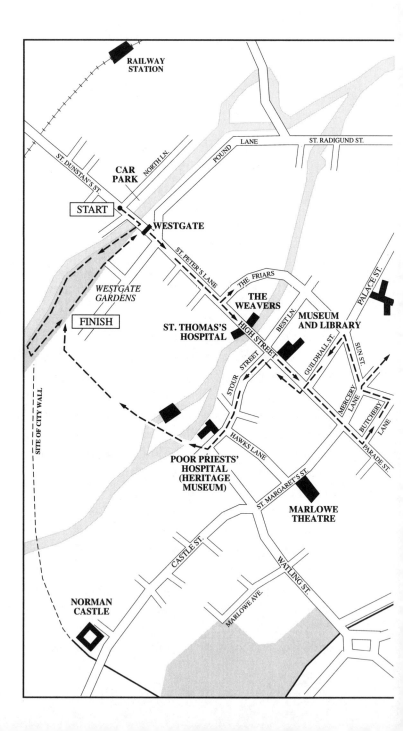

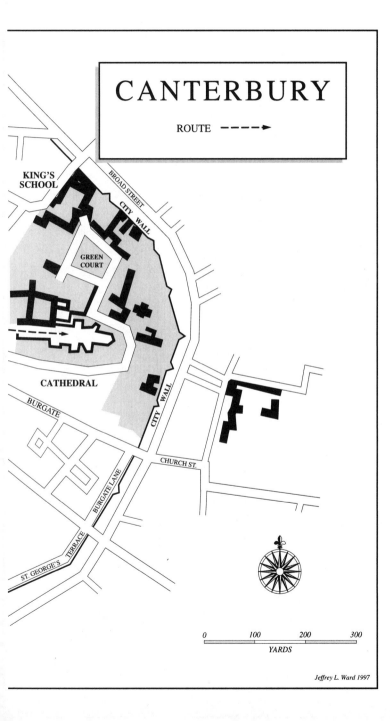

CANTERBURY

ROUTE -----▶

KING'S
SCHOOL

BROAD STREET

CITY WALL

GREEN
COURT

CATHEDRAL

BURGATE

CITY WALL

BURGATE LANE

CHURCH ST.

ST. GEORGE'S TERRACE

0   100   200   300
YARDS

Jeffrey L. Ward 1997

although the magnificent Cathedral is reason enough for your visit, Canterbury is filled with many other interesting places—the old city wall, a medieval hostel for pilgrims, and sixteenth-century houses once occupied by Walloon and Huguenot weavers—to mention only a few. The road through the heart of Canterbury has recently been closed to cars. So now visitors can stroll at leisure past the ancient inns and modern gift shops of this thriving tourist town. Once more the main sounds of Canterbury are the chatter of conversation, the playing of street musicians, and the footsteps of countless people heading toward the cathedral close.

You should start this walk through Canterbury at the massive twin-turreted **Westgate,** the historic and only remaining gateway into the city. But before you approach the Westgate, glance at the delightful, though modestly maintained three-storied red brick Georgian building, **Westgate House,** opposite the **Falstaff Hotel.** There are wooden shutters at the ground floor windows, and the original drainpipes wander upward. Look for the date 1760 molded at the head of each pipe. Plain, dignified, flat-fronted buildings like this are found in most of the English towns which had prosperity in the Georgian era.

Rebuilt by Archbishop Sudbury about 1380 on Roman and Norman foundations, the gray stone Westgate stands at the strategic crossing of the **River Stour.** Look for the arrow-slits and observation-holes in the stonework. Here goods brought from the Continent and landed at Kentish ports were transported into the city. Today cars squeeze through the narrow arch where Henry II made his way to the Cathedral "barefoot and weeping" in 1174 to do penance for the murder of Archbishop Thomas Becket. In later centuries, Chaucer and the Canterbury pilgrims probably passed through this gate.

Go to the right under the arch, on a small piece of pavement next to the traffic. You will see an ancient door, fortified with iron studs.

In a moment, go through it and up the winding stone staircase. But first notice the rusting iron supports on which the city's gates once swung, and the slot under the arch to let the portcullis drop in an emergency. Now go upstairs to the little **Westgate Museum** (open 11:00–12:30; 1:30–3:30, Monday–Saturday). Check whether you can buy a single ticket to let you into all of the city's museums, including this one: this is much cheaper than paying each time. This was the city prison from 1400 to 1829. You will see prisoners' cells with convicts' chains and irons. The armory includes helmets and weapons from the seventeenth-century civil wars, as well as a collection of constables' truncheons used by the early police forces during the Chartist riots in 1843. There is also a wooden noise-maker, used by police to summon help, one hundred years before the coming of the two-way radio. Public executions were done here. Look at the top of the tall window in the main room of the museum. There is a small wooden hatch: this was to allow placement of a beam from which the rope and the victim would hang. The city gate was chosen for executions because here people converged in the greatest numbers, and the straight roads let them see from afar. Hanging was supposed to be an improving spectacle, to discipline the citizenry.

Go farther up the winding stair, to reach the roof. From here is a lovely panorama of the city. Looking toward the towers of the cathedral you see the main pilgrims' route, which you will walk shortly. Why the medieval pilgrims? Becket's death in 1170, instigated by a king, stood as a dreadful reminder to the medieval church of the power of the secular authority. The cult of Becket was promoted by the church as a standing reminder to royalty that any repetition would be massively unpopular. No wonder that when Henry VIII moved against the church he dismantled the shrine of Becket.

Once back downstairs in the street, cross the main road (with great care; the Westgate obstructs your view of traffic) for a stroll through the **Westgate Gardens** on the banks of the Stour. At the entrance you will see on the opposite side of the river **timber and stucco houses** in characteristic Tudor style with overhanging upper stories. These were at one time inns for pilgrims. The gardens built on the foundations of the Roman walls are particularly attractive because of their fine trees (especially an oriental plane, with a huge trunk, about two hundred years old), beautiful roses, and lawns like putting greens. Rose trellises along the river banks and the branches of the trees dipping into the stream make this one of the loveliest walks in Canterbury. Look for trout, hovering above the strings of waterweed which sway in the stream.

On your return to the Westgate, turn right, walk for one hundred fifty yards, then turn left into **St. Peter's Lane.** You will see immediately, ahead of you, a superb Georgian house, with a fanlight over the door, a plant climbing the wall, and a colorful walled garden in front. Brass plates outside show that this is a dentists' surgery. Rarely can the path to a dentist's be so appealing. Go back onto the main street, St. Peter's. Turn left, then after about twenty yards look right at the façade of a **Methodist church** of 1811. Methodist buildings were usually rather plain, on principle: splendor was the mark of their high church rivals, a distraction from true spirituality. But this tall building is an exception. It is magnificent. The bricks, now newly cleaned, are yellowish fawn. The elaborate fanlight above the door catches the eye of the traveler in the main street, as it was surely meant to. This building was the Methodists' answer to Canterbury Cathedral. With the Anglicans possessed of so fine a structure, the Methodist church had to compete. Rivalry between these two faiths in Georgian times was intense. Conservative employers would dismiss their employees for joining the Methodists. The Methodists were seen as subversive of political as well as religious authority. Ironically, political historians now suspect that it was Methodism which prevented revolution in nineteenth-century

Britain, by diverting the masses from earthly ambitions to the quest for eternal reward. As socialist agitators said despairingly, "Pie in the sky when you die." (By the early twentieth century, according to George Orwell, religion had ceased to be the great opiate of the British masses. In his view, what may have prevented revolution in 1920s England was the drinking of tea.)

Walk farther along St. Peter's Street for about one hundred yards, to a small bridge over an arm of the River Stour. On your left, on the edge of the river, stands the old house called **The Weavers.** Stand on the bridge and look at these gabled half-timbered houses that rise above the river. They were built in 1500 for French-speaking Protestant weavers who sought refuge in England from religious persecution. The interior is now a gift shop. Signs nearby direct you to boat tours on the river.

A few steps farther, across St. Peter's Street, is the old **St. Thomas's Hospital,** set up in the twelfth century to lodge poor or sick pilgrims. Go down to the crypt, with its lovely Norman arches. This was the pilgrims' dormitory. Then go upstairs to the former refectory and look for the faded but handsome religious wall paintings from the twelfth and thirteenth centuries.

One hundred fifty yards farther along the main street (now called **High Street**), on the right, is the fine Tudor building called **Queen Elizabeth's Guest Chamber,** now a restaurant. In Tudor days, this was the state room of the Crown Inn, one of the principal inns for pilgrims. Here in 1573, according to local lore, Queen Elizabeth I received one of her suitors, the French Duke of Alençon. You will admire the fine sixteenth-century plaster ceiling with the initials "E.R." in the second-story restaurant.

Another one hundred fifty yards along the main street, turn left into **Butchery Lane.** Halfway down this narrow street, on the right, are modern columns at the entrance to the **Roman Museum.** This contains many domestic and religious objects from the Roman town. The reason for the museum's existence in this spot, you will see in the basement. Bombing during World War II, which destroyed much of old Canterbury, blew open the foundations of a building here to reveal a fine Roman mosaic; further excavation then revealed parts of a luxurious Roman town house. Look for the short columns of tiles which supported the raised floor, allowing hot air from a furnace to circulate and heat the room above.

Walk to the far end of Butchery Lane and turn left into **Burgate.** In less than one hundred yards you will be in one of the finest spots in any English town, the little square called **Butter Market.** On one side are ancient timbered buildings, on the other stands the majestic stonework of **Christchurch Gate,** the main entrance to the cathedral precinct. This Tudor gateway, dating from 1517, is ornamented with brilliantly colored and gilded crests. Admire the elaborate carving on the seventeenth-century wooden gates.

Canterbury Cathedral, spiritual home of the Anglican Church, stands near the site of St. Augustine's Cathedral which was dedicated in 602, five years after the baptism of the Saxon King Ethelbert of Kent. During the next four hundred years, a second cathedral was erected after the destruction of St. Augustine's, only to be consumed by fire in 1067. The third and present cathedral was begun by the Norman Archbishop Lanfranc in 1070. Though much of the cathedral as it remains today was constructed during the eleventh and twelfth centuries, alterations and additions have taken place throughout the centuries up to the present.

Before entering the cathedral, stroll about **the precincts** a few minutes so you can appreciate the glory of its exterior, the **twin towers** at the west entrance and the magnificent two hundred fifty-foot **Bell Harry Tower,** with its slim windows, one of the finest Gothic towers ever built.

Starting at the **southwest entrance,** you will be impressed by the majestic sweep of the nave. Its lofty piers rise to the graceful vaulting in the roof, which is decorated by superbly carved stone bosses, one of the cathedral's great art treasures. As you walk toward the steps leading to the choir, turn back to view the **west window.** The glass in its lower tiers dates back to the late twelfth and early thirteenth century. At the end of the nave, go left and down steps to the reputed site of Becket's murder. A dramatic modern sculpture represents the swords with which the will of Henry II was done. From here, more steps lead down to the vast, quiet **crypt.**

Back at the east end of the nave, go to the center of the building, and look far above you to the fan vaulting and the superb decorations of gold, red, and blue in the ceiling of Bell Harry Tower. After you pass the choir, continue along the south aisle to the **Trinity Chapel** at the eastern end of the cathedral. On the way you will pass a case with the original armor, including helmet, that belonged to the Black Prince. Up the steps in the center behind the High Altar is the Trinity Chapel. Here once stood the shrine of St. Thomas, the focus of the Canterbury pilgrimages for over three hundred years, until Henry VIII intervened. You can see the grooves in the pavement made by the thousands of pilgrims who knelt there.

A few yards away, on the south side of the chapel, is the **brass effigy and tomb** of the Black Prince (died 1376); notice the spurs and knuckle-dusters. In the circular apse, beneath the thirteenth-century glass windows portraying St. Thomas's miracles, stands **St. Augustine's marble chair.** It is used by every Archbishop of Canterbury when he is enthroned.

On coming out of the cathedral, go round to the west end once more. As you turn to pass the **west towers,** notice the headless statues set in the cathedral wall—the damage was done, no doubt, by puritan soldiers in the mid-seventeenth century, protesting against the high church use of icons. Walk round to the far, north, side of the cathedral to explore the fifteenth-century **cloister,** with its collection of coats of arms in the vaulting. Stop in at the **Chapter House** to see its fine roof. You will see the **Archbishop's palace** just above the cloisters. His flag flies when he is in residence.

Go back through Christchurch Gate to the Butter Market and turn right into **Sun Street.** At the first corner on the left you will see the reason for the street's name. Here stands, with lovely old red brick and timber in its upper section, the former **Sun Hotel** (reputedly established in 1503), one of the many pubs mentioned by Charles Dickens. Go left here, and left again into **Guildhall Street.** Where this street joins the main High Street, look fifteen feet up on the wall of High Street which faces down Guildhall Street. Some obsolete traffic signs are deliberately left here, pointing to Dover and Chatham, from the unlamented days—only a few years past—when this was an arterial road for motor traffic.

Back down High Street in the direction of Westgate are some alluring pubs, as you will have noticed earlier. Look for one selling the famous bitter beer brewed by the Kentish firm of Shepherd Neame. Hops, for making beer, are a traditional crop in Kent. On your way back from Canterbury notice in the fields, next to farmhouses, small, circular, brick buildings with conical roofs. These are, or rather were, oast houses—kilns for drying the hops.

On a summer day, a pleasant alternative route to return to Westgate and the railway station is through the backstreets and gardens. From Guildhall Street, turn right into High Street and then second left into quiet **Stour Street.** About two hundred yards along Stour Street, on the right, is the **Canterbury Heritage Museum.** Look in for three treasures. There is a portable miniature sundial, to fit in the hand, made in Anglo-Saxon times. A Viking bone-handled knife shows that the folding mechanism of penknives was used in the tenth century. And oldest and most spectacular is the recently discovered Canterbury Pendant from c. A.D. 600—magnificent Anglo-Saxon work, made of garnets set in gold, in the style made famous by the Sutton Hoo treasure. Look also for the many metal badges, about two inches high, sold to medieval pilgrims and bearing the effigy of Thomas Becket. They have pins on the back, like a modern button. These tourist souvenirs reveal how closely modern Canterbury echoes the medieval city.

Immediately beyond the museum turn right onto a narrow footpath which will lead you through gardens and across bridges. (After the first bridge explore on the right for Grey Friars Friary.) Back on your path you will cross two sleepy terraces of little houses, and then one busier road. Signs along the way direct you toward Westgate Gardens. Once in the gardens, turn right and you will recognize the Westgate where the walk began.

Phone: Tourist Information, Canterbury: 01227-766567

☙ CHICHESTER

The cathedral city of **Chichester,** one of the most interesting and attractive places in southern England, lies in the flat country between Sussex's South Downs and the sea. As you step off the train from London, your first impression may be of a special quality in the light: that brightness is from the sea. The streets around the town center are now mainly for pedestrians. You can walk around the historic parts of the town in peace. Peace, in fact, is a theme of Chichester, from its earliest history to the present. When the Romans began their settlement of Britain, in A.D. 43, the local ruler in these parts, Cogidubnus, obliged them (and spited his enemies) by collaborating with a will. As a result he kept his kingdom, was made an honorary senator of Rome, and lived in some splendor. The extensive ruins of his palace have been uncovered in recent years at **Fishbourne,** at the edge of Chichester. In more recent times, Chichester has been dominated by its cathedral and clerics. The result is quiet streets, well preserved old buildings on a homely scale, and any number of beautiful walled gardens, many of them in the shadow of the cathedral.

The Roman influence is reflected in the plan of the city, with four main streets and city walls. **The walls,** which circle the old town for a mile and a half, are built on Roman foundations though the visible sections are largely medieval.

Begin your stroll through Chichester at the town's center, the **Market Cross,** the junction of the four streets, appropriately named North, South, East, and West. Here the poor of Chichester sold their wares until 1808. The graceful cross, presented to the city in 1501 and regarded as the finest of its kind in England, is built of carved Caen stone in the shape of an open-arcaded octagon. Fifty feet high, the elaborate façade with its shields and other decoration is supported by huge buttresses. Pinnacles rise above the arches and an octagonal cupola surmounts the graceful medieval structure. Beneath the cupola there is the city's main clock. Years ago the arcade sheltered country people when they came to town.

From the Market Cross turn into **West Street.** On the right, twenty-five yards along, look at the handsome Georgian exterior of the **Dolphin and Anchor Hotel** (and coffee shop). This was a coaching inn. Look into its cobbled yard, where horses and carriages once clattered. Boxing matches and cockfights were held here, in the bare-knuckled eighteenth century.

Now cross the road toward the **cathedral.** The saying "Happy is the land with no history," applies well to Chichester. In spite of its prosperity, it seems never to have produced any individual generally remembered in Britain. The closest it came was with the invention, in this spot beside the cathedral, of a homely and very popular fish-paste, Shippams. The cottage in which the fish boiling was done was demolished in the 1850s, no doubt to the relief of the clergy, and replaced with decorous lime trees. The factory moved to a more discreet part of town.

From here is perhaps the finest view of the cathedral. The stone is pale yellow. On the first story are gothic windows. Above them,

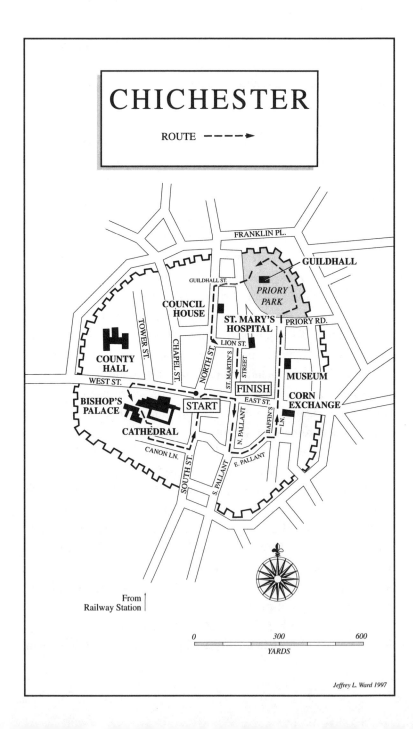

close to the massive buttresses, the windows are Norman—rounded with dogtooth decoration. Look up to the tall spire (some two hundred seventy-seven feet high). This is a fairly modern replacement. A Victorian traveler was looking from his train in 1861 and got a surprise. One moment the spire was there; then it had gone. It had collapsed into the nave.

Go farther along the side of the cathedral to a rare feature—a free-standing **medieval bell tower.** Weather-beaten, it stands some forty-five feet from the cathedral. Look to the cathedral wall opposite the bell tower for the gargoyles. Water spouts project from their mouths, to direct the rain from the gutters away from the walls.

Essentially a Norman building, the main part of the cathedral was constructed during the early years of the twelfth century. The double aisles of the **nave,** one of the cathedral's most distinctive features, make it one of the widest in the country. From the entrance turn right into the south aisle. Thirty yards along, set in the wall on the right, is a beautiful Elizabethan brass showing husband and wife at prayer. Behind him are their six sons; behind her, their eight daughters.

Go right for a moment into the **south transept** to look at paintings of English monarchs made in the reign of Henry VIII. It is said that the damage to the eye in the painting of Edward VI, bottom right, was done by a puritan soldier during the civil wars. Walk farther along the main south wall to view rare **twelfth-century sculptures,** in the romanesque style, showing Lazarus and Christ. A few feet away part of the floor of the aisle has been replaced by glass, to reveal part of a **Roman mosaic** beneath. Here once was the town house of a wealthy Romano-Briton.

At the very end of this aisle, facing you, is the cathedral's modern treasure—a dramatic **painting by Graham Sutherland.** It shows the risen Christ with Mary Magdalene. The treatment of the subject is distinctively twentieth century; sexuality is a prominent theme.

Magdalene, the reformed prostitute, puts her hand on Christ's thigh, but he directs her ambition to heaven, with raised arm. The artist's intention is made very clear by the unrealistic emphasis he gives, cartoon-style, to the woman's breasts and bottom. The title of the picture is "Noli me tangere": "Don't touch me."

On leaving, step across for a moment to the garden of the **Prebendal School,** opposite the cathedral's main entrance. Now walk to the cathedral's south side—the side away from the bell tower—and go through a door into the fifteenth-century cloisters. Thirty yards along the cloister, on the right, is the refectory café, strongly recommended for the tranquil walled garden in which customers may sit. Come back twenty yards, in the same part of the cloister, and turn into **St. Richard's Walk** to a delightful part of the precinct. Look for "flinting"—the local custom of coating walls in small flints. There is a quiet, otherworldly air along these walks behind the cathedral. **Medieval and Georgian houses,** with their flower-covered walls, big trees, and tastefully planted gardens, make this part behind the cathedral one of the most delightful sections of Chichester. Though you are only yards from the busy main streets and shopping area, you seem to be miles away as you poke about these fascinating corners of the close.

Starting down St. Richard's Walk from the cloisters, the **flint building** on your left (No. 1) is the house of the Wiccamical Prebendaries and dates from the fourteenth century. No. 2, an eighteenth-century house, is most attractive. High stone walls line the walk to **Canon Lane.** Just across is **The Deanery,** a distinguished red brick eighteenth-century house. Turn right along Canon Lane for a few yards to the fourteenth-century gatehouse of the **Bishop's Palace.** If you step through the arch for a few moments you will see the large stone palace, part of which was built in the thirteenth century. Go left into the next section of the garden. In sunshine this is a magic spot. A high garden wall of faded red brick gives privacy and reflects heat, as you look over flowers to the kitchen garden beyond.

Now stroll back down Canon Lane beneath high stone walls and past the Deanery. The building on your right is the **Residentiary,** mostly of the sixteenth century. Farther down on the right is the thirteenth-century **Chantry,** older than any other domestic building in Chichester. Look for the irregular roof and the stone gothic arches in the windows. Directly opposite is **Blackman House** with a fine Georgian fanlight above the door. On your left before you go through the thirteenth-century Canon Gate to South Street, you will find the **Vicars' Close** with four fifteenth-century houses. In front are well-kept cottage gardens. Rose trees climb the walls.

Turn left in **South Street** past some interesting shops. In a few moments you will come to the **Vicars' Hall and Undercroft.** Go down into the Undercroft, now a restaurant, for a snack or lunch. You'll find it quite amusing to eat in this vaulted twelfth-century crypt which, next to the Cathedral, is the "oldest visible remnant of medieval architecture in the city." It is believed that the crypt or undercroft was part of one of the ancient Guildhalls. Go upstairs for a look at the fourteenth-century Vicars' Hall with its **open timber roof.**

Walk up South Street for another look at the Market Cross, then go right on **East Street.** Turn right on **North Pallant. The Pallants**—North, South, East, and West—are a miniature version of Chichester's streets of the same name. The word "Pallant" comes from the Latin *"palantia"* meaning exclusive jurisdiction and signifies the fact that the Archbishop of Canterbury had such rights in this area until the middle of the sixteenth century. As you stroll down North Pallant you'll see that the houses on this and the other Pallants are of unusually fine proportions with most attractive doorways and windows. Look for the finely carved porches, and for the different "lights"—fanlights and other designs—above the doors of nos. 4, 5, 6, 14, and 17. On a dark night, before the days of public street lighting, the distinctive pattern illuminated above the door could help visitors find the right house. Few of these houses are still private residences. Most were erected during the eighteenth and early nineteenth centuries. The large brick house at the corner of North and East Pallants is **Pallant House,** built in about 1712. It is familiarly known as Dodo House, from the stone ostriches, which stand perched on the brick gatepiers, the crest of the original owner. The fine interior of the house, with a small art collection, is now open to visitors. Go twenty yards diagonally opposite, to the corner of West Pallant—for the view of the cathedral spire in the distance, above this Georgian street.

Walk into East Pallant, by the side of Dodo House, and look through the stylish metal gate into the garden. Here are honey-suckle, ornate lead water tanks from the eighteenth century, and a magnificent window. Then walk on to **Baffin's Lane,** turn left and go to the junction with busy **East Street.** Here, on the corner at the right, stand massive and handsome Doric columns—the entrance to the **Corn Exchange** (built 1830). Corn (i.e., wheat) was a source of great wealth to landowners at the time. (The profitable export of it from Ireland to England had devastating effects on the Irish food supply.) The near-religious veneration of this golden commodity helps explain the solemn style of the building, in imitation of a Greek temple. Here the corn was auctioned. Today the Corn Exchange is used for the sale of another food, similarly profitable, charismatic, and controversial. Above the Doric columns, discreet but highly visible, is a new gold—the golden arches of McDonald's.

Cross East Street and, almost directly opposite the Corn Exchange, enter **Little London.** About one hundred fifty yards along this street, past eighteenth-century houses, is the **City Museum** (open Tuesday–Saturday, 10:00–5:30). The museum's collection covers the history of Chichester from prehistoric times to the present. Its well displayed exhibits include an extensive collection of Roman relics—vases, coins, glass, jewelry, etc.—as well as many pieces from the Saxon and medieval periods of the city's history. Look for the moveable stocks. This engine of punishment for petty offenders was built on a trolley to be wheeled around from parish to parish. Its last recorded use was in 1852. Also of note are eighteenth-century cartoons of smuggling, a considerable industry at the time along the coast of Sussex, far from big towns and close to France.

From the museum continue along Little London to **Priory Road** where you turn right past a fine mansion and cross into the park. Keep to your right along the park and go up on the walk that runs along the top of the **old city wall.** It's a delightful stroll under the trees with a park on either side. In a few minutes you will pass a high grassy mound, the remains of Chichester Castle. To control the beaten Anglo-Saxons, a timber keep—a primitive form of castle— was built here soon after 1066, at the order of Roger de Montgomery, a leading henchman of William the Conqueror. The Montgomery family, at this period, acquired large tracts of Britain. In A.D. 1102 they had enough land to stage a coup against the third Norman king, Henry I. The coup failed. The family lost most of their lands. Symbolically, their former **castle mound** now sleeps neglected, barely marked, and visited by few, under its chestnut trees.

The stone building set back on the lawn is the **Guildhall,** all that remains of a medieval Franciscan monastery. Leave the park by the gates near the Guildhall. The brick gateposts are each surmounted by the wreck of an eighteenth-century oil lamp. Walk fifty yards along **Guildhall Street,** opposite the gates, to the **Ship Hotel** on the right. From this street notice its lovely oval Georgian windows. It is worth having a drink at this prosperous hotel to see (opposite the reception desk) the seating plan of a dinner given here, on 21st April 1944. The guest of honor was General Eisenhower. His hosts were the RAF. D-Day was imminent, which helps to explain Eisenhower's presence here on the south coast. Look at the names of the senior air force officers present. Many are Polish, a reminder of the large part played in the war by exiled Polish troops—something often forgotten. Eisenhower lodged here from the 19th to the 22nd of April. The hotel's number is given below, in case you wish to follow in his footsteps.

If you were to go right on North Street for about ten minutes or so, you would come to the **Chichester Festival Theatre** where Sir Laurence Olivier directed the National Theatre in its opening productions. Its summer seasons, a major element in British drama, are famous internationally.

A few yards to the left along North Street from Guildhall Street will bring you to the **Council House** with its open arcade over the sidewalk. Before you go in, notice the famous **stone** with an inscription dedicating a temple to Neptune and Minerva, an important relic of Roman days. By looking closely you can still make out most of the name of Cogidubnus, the Celtic king of this area who cooperated with the Romans. The inscription mentions the Divine House, i.e., the ruling family of Rome, so probably it dates from the A.D. 50s or 60s, during the reign of the somewhat megalomanic emperor Nero. (After A.D. 69, the authorities in Rome turned their backs for a while on claims to supernatural status. When the emperor Vespasian was dying in A.D. 79, he said, "I think I am turning into a god!" and meant it as a joke.) The façade of the eighteenth-century brick building with its white Ionic columns has a particularly graceful air.

Walk a few yards farther along the same side of North Street to the columns of the **Butter Market,** built in 1807 to the designs of the court architect John Nash. Then retrace your steps and immediately after the Council House, turn right into **Lion Street** and walk along it to lovely, sleepy, **St. Martin's Square.** Look for the elegant fanlight above the door of No. 2, and for the brick porch at No. 3.

Across the square is **St. Mary's Hospital,** founded in the thirteenth century. It is now an almshouse for old women of Chichester. Turn right, along **St. Martin's Street,** looking into the first gateway for a walled garden well stocked with flowers. You are now heading back toward the center of the town and the Market Cross. Many pleasant pubs are nearby. For "a good pint," as the British say, try the *Hogshead Pub* in South Street (on the left as you head for the railway station). The pub has an excellent selection of bitters.

Useful phone numbers:
Tourist Information, Chichester: 01243 775888
Ship Hotel, Chichester, 01243 788000

⚘ Church Stretton

We have chosen **Church Stretton** in Shropshire as one of the most characteristic and yet untrafficked English villages. It lies in a deep valley, and feels out of the world. One side of the valley is the wooded hill called **Wenlock Edge.** On the other is a gentle mountain, the **Long Mynd** (pronounced "minnd"). Our route ends with directions to the top of the mountain seventeen hundred feet up. If you wish, this can be made an ambitious walk. (Bring waterproof garments, in case the weather changes.) The village is, on its own, a delightful, satisfying, and restful place to explore. Treat the mountain as an extra, to tackle if energy and weather allow.

You'll find Church Stretton is border country. In the Middle Ages, English and Welsh invaded each other hereabouts. The word "Mynd" is Welsh for mountain. In more recent times, for English people in the plains of the industrial Midlands looking westward to the sunset, these hills of Shropshire were, as the poet A. E. Housman put it, "the blue, remembered hills." For Shropshire people among those hills, the romantic uplands of imagination are still farther west:

those of Wales itself. Housman wrote, thinking of the final expulsion of the Welsh from Shropshire:

> *The vanquished eve, as night prevails,*
> *Bleeds upon the road to Wales.*

You will understand, in the lovely setting of Church Stretton, why this land should have been so long contested.

The town has a railway station, on the line from Manchester and Crewe (in northwest England) and from Cardiff in South Wales. From the station, walk left into **Sandford Avenue,** one of the two main shopping streets of the village. Turn left for a moment into **Easthope Road;** just inside this street, on the left, is a faded but distinguished industrial building in red brick—a former malthouse. The beam from which a pulley once hung can still be seen, high above you. Come back, left, into Sandford Avenue and walk to the crossroads where stand two banks, which date from the period after World War I. Go straight across, into **Burway Road.** Forty yards along, on the right, look over the six-foot stone wall for the orchard and cottage gardens that lie behind.

After the orchard wall, take the first right, **Longhills Road.** After a few yards bear left onto a footpath which goes steeply uphill and passes, some ten yards away to the left, a small **shelter** of wood and slate, with a pointed roof, designed to give a view of the village. For an even better view, go a few yards farther uphill to the tall **stone cross** which is a memorial to the village's dead in two world wars. From the war memorial look over the roofs of the village and its church tower, and across the valley to the wooded slopes of Wenlock Edge.

After facing the church tower, look right to the rich gardens below you. Even at midday there is birdsong in the peaceful woods here. Behind towering fir trees stands the former rectory. Countless

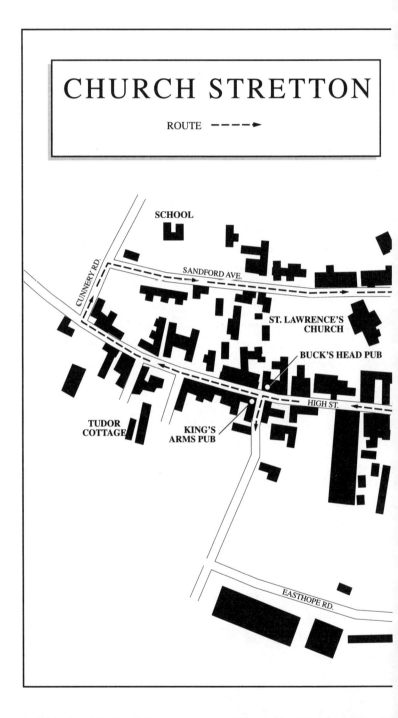

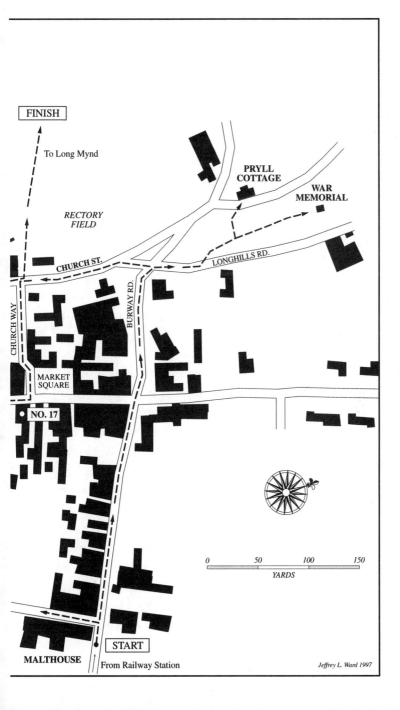

FINISH

To Long Mynd

RECTORY
FIELD

PRYLL
COTTAGE

WAR
MEMORIAL

CHURCH ST.

LONGHILLS RD.

BURWAY RD.

CHURCH WAY

MARKET
SQUARE

NO. 17

0   50   100   150
YARDS

START

MALTHOUSE   From Railway Station

Jeffrey L. Ward 1997

English villages contain a splendid mansion like this, from Georgian or Victorian times, when the rector, the local Anglican priest, was a member of the landed gentry. In recent years the Church of England has, from policy, sold many of these buildings and moved its clergy into ordinary houses, in an attempt to gain contact with ordinary people. The church has ceased to be what it was for centuries: "the Tory party at prayer." Now on the gravelled drives of the Old Rectories of England there is no longer the rattle of vicars' bicycles, but the purr of Jaguar and Range Rover: the sounds of the Tory party at play.

Turn right for a moment onto the lane which runs ten yards below the shelter, to see **Pryll Cottage.** Flowering plants climb the building. Just beyond, is a high wall in red brick to capture warmth for the cottage garden. Now come back, past the two pine trees on your left, and turn right into **Church Street,** heading for the church tower. Before the church, look over the stone wall into the garden of a fine house with small, gothic windows, set in its own orchard. There are flowering shrubs around its ornate, glazed porch.

Immediately before the churchyard, turn left down **Church Way,** which brings you to the little market square. Decoration in the black-and-white "half-timbered" style is much in evidence here. The most distinguished building, on a pleasantly human scale, is facing you: **No. 17 High Street.** Down the corners of this Queen Anne building (c. 1700) of red brick runs a pattern of stone blocks. Cross to it, passing the market stalls, and go down the little lane immediately to the right of the house. Here, and not on the main road, is the front door, with a beautiful carved porch and a satisfying fanlight. Ten yards farther along the lane, on the left, you may see a bush of honeysuckle growing over a wall from the courtyard behind. A few yards beyond are pleasant, modernized cottages. These ancient **alleyways,** turning from the main street, are a delightful feature of Church Stretton. Come back to the Queen Anne house, turn left into **High Street** and explore for a moment the next alley on the left; look again for the mellowed red brick, the neglected glory of old buildings in the English Midlands. Back into High Street again. This street was once part of the coaching road from Shrewsbury to Bristol. Travelers and business people needed hotels and refreshment—which helps to explain some of the stylish buildings in the village from before the railway age.

Farther along High Street, on the right is the **Buck's Head pub.** Built in austerely pleasant red brick in 1868, it has stone facings to its corners and windows. Immediately after the Buck's Head, go right for five yards, to look over the back of the churchyard to the bank of trees beyond. Then come back, turn right into High Street once more, and walk until you are opposite the **King's Arms pub.** This is a splendid place, an example of the English pub at its best: intimate, unpretentious, historic. Explore its setting before you go in. Immediately before the pub, go down the alley. On your right is the ancient, timbered wall of the pub—look back in a moment to see how it bows outward from age. The building seems to date from the late 1500s. On the left of the alley is **Insurance House,** another lovely old dwelling house with its front door—and fine fanlight—in the alley. Go farther down the winding alley, then look over the wall on the right to see the **beer garden** of the King's Arms—a peaceful, walled garden with a lawn and small trees. Now come back to High Street, to enter the pub itself. You will see that, unlike many pubs, the interior has not been stereotyped. There is still wooden paneling and a continuous seat almost the length of the wall. Ancient black beams run across the ceiling. Look in the corner, to the left of the door as you enter, for a framed copy of a summons (subpoena) issued to a resident here in 1926, to be witness in the case of a drunk being in charge of a horse. The traditional bitter beers are the ones served by vertical hand pump. You may also find home cooking. In good weather, look for the passage through to the beer garden.

Leaving the pub, farther along High Street and just before the large Victorian chapel on the left, is **Ragleth House.** This is a Georgian gem, small but distinguished. Look at the intricate doorway, with fanlight, carvings, and molding. In Victorian times the house was used as a girls' boarding school, run by four sisters. Thirty yards beyond the chapel stands a splendid antique: **Tudor Cottage,** seemingly built about 1600. For the best view of this black-and-white, timbered building, cross to the opposite side of High Street, from where you can see the signs of age, the irregularities in its walls and roof. Just beyond Tudor Cottage, where bungalows are now, there once stood a private Lunatic Asylum for Gentlemen. Whether for boarding schools or for the mentally ill, Church Stretton was seen in the nineteenth century as a place that gave shelter. The reason, no doubt, was its position in a deep, sunlit, valley away from towns.

Opposite Tudor Cottage, walk twenty-five yards up **Cunnery Road** then turn right into **Church Street.** One hundred yards along, on the left, is a classic Victorian village school, in Gothic architecture. It now houses the **Tourist Information office:** call in for advice, maps, or literature. Its number is given below. Walk on to the **church of St. Lawrence,** which you approached from the opposite direction early in the walk. If you have visited some of the mighty cathedrals described on other walks, this small, medieval building—the typical church of an English village—will make a pleasant contrast. Look inside for the impressive roof beams and the simple stone walls. Outside, facing the main door, turn left and go a few yards to the far, north side of the church. Here is a **Norman doorway,** with rounded arches above. Look up, perhaps eighteen inches above the arches, for an interesting non-Christian symbol. This is a small medieval stone statue of a human female, legs apart and displaying her genitals. Statues of this kind are common in Ireland and are known by the Irish name Sheila na Gig ("Sheila of the breasts"). In recent years they have been hailed as a long-overlooked element of old Irish culture. Some conservative people in Ireland, in love with the idea of the Land of Saints and Scholars, would have preferred the Sheila na Gigs to be overlooked for a while longer.

From the Norman doorway, walk to the metal stile in the nearest corner of the churchyard. Cross the stile and five yards farther, diagonally to your left across Church Street, is the entrance to **Rectory Field.** Walk in; on the right is a distant view across a meadow, of the Old Rectory, with its austerely beautiful, creeper-clad façade.

You are now on a public footpath to the top of the **Long Mynd.** Why go up the mountain? There are views which you will remember for years, not just of the Stretton valley, but over much of western Britain, from the Cheshire plains in the north to the Black Mountains of Wales in the south. The walk to the top takes between an hour and ninety minutes, across easy terrain all the way. The journey down takes half that time. If going right to the top seems too much, most of the fine views can be had from halfway up. And the walk makes a wonderful prelude to an hour or two in the garden of the King's Arms!

If the weather is fine and you decide to go, keep in mind that at the top of the mountain the weather could change very quickly. Walk directly ahead from the gate, across Rectory Field and uphill; on each side are woods, and you walk up the broad field between them. At the top of the field a long brick wall runs across, to left and right. The wall is the boundary of **Tiger Hall,** built with crenellated towers and verandah to recall the British Raj in India. Go left; where the wall ends, leave the field and turn sharp right into the road which leads past the entrance to Tiger Hall. About one hundred yards beyond the Hall, on the right, is a sign saying "**Public Footpath to Town Brook Hollow.**" (Signs sometimes disappear; just in case, the footpath starts immediately before the bungalow named "Woodlands.") Turn right, onto the footpath, which leads you up steep steps through a wood. At the top of the steps is a stile: cross it and take the footpath to the right. Go along this path, slightly uphill, for about seventy paces, then, just where the path starts to go downhill, go left up a steep, stony zigzag path for about ten yards, then sharp left onto a broad, grassy path which will take you toward the ridge. There are many gentle routes to the top. Before you choose one, look back now to memorize your approximate position with respect to the wood you have just left, and to Church Stretton beyond. This will help you navigate on the way back.

As you cross the open hillside, look for small, sparrowlike birds with white outer tail feathers, fluttering away from you out of the bracken, then diving back into it. These are meadow pipits, cousins of the skylark. In spring they climb into the air and then parachute gently down, singing.

Look back toward Church Stretton. You will recognize Wenlock Edge, with its woods, just beyond the village and to the right. Far away to the north (your left), at the opposite end of the same ridge as Wenlock Edge, is the sharp hill called **The Wrekin.** Its name comes from Viroconium, a Roman town close by. Now that the long, straight valley of Church Stretton lies clear before you, it's easy to see why the Romans made a road along it. The name of Stretton comes from this road—Latin *"strata"* (paved road). Beyond the Wrekin are the plains of Shropshire and Cheshire; beyond them (out of sight) are the cities of Manchester and Liverpool. Eastward again, behind Wenlock Edge, you see the Malvern Hills of Worcestershire. And south, to your right, are the distant Black Mountains of Wales.

Phone: Tourist Information office, Church Stretton: 01694 723133

DORCHESTER ✦

This lively country town is set among some of the most peaceful and satisfying countryside in England. A few yards from the main pedestrian street, quiet lanes lead toward the gentle **River Frome.** Historic buildings, relatively seldom visited, are everywhere. They are carefully preserved, but not in an overelaborate way. This is historic England as it was, rather than some exquisitely framed period piece.

Dorchester and its countryside were the home and the imaginative setting used by the novelist Thomas Hardy. Here, during his long, fairly happy, and very successful life (1840–1928) Hardy created scenes of pathos amid rural landscapes of painful beauty. Love-gone-wrong was a favorite theme. In the splendor of nearby Blackmore Vale a heroine watches, at sunset, as the white horse of her husband dwindles to a dot in the distance—as it carries him away to his lover (in *The Woodlanders*). In Dorchester itself, Hardy set the tragedy of Mayor Henchard, who in temper renounces his wife, then spends his ruined life regretting it. That is in *The Mayor*

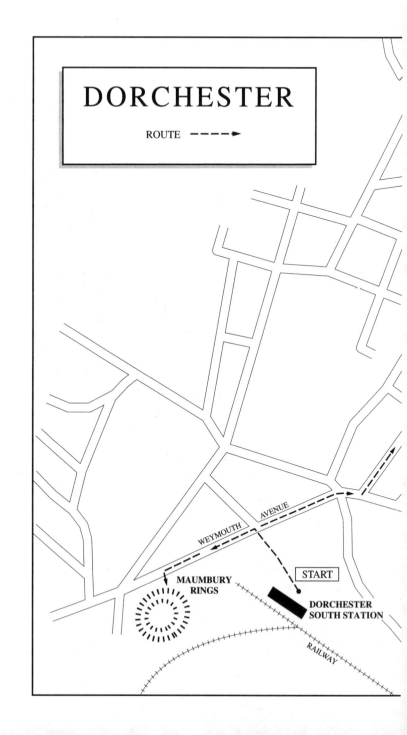

DORCHESTER

ROUTE ------▶

AVENUE

WEYMOUTH

MAUMBURY
RINGS

START

DORCHESTER
SOUTH STATION

RAILWAY

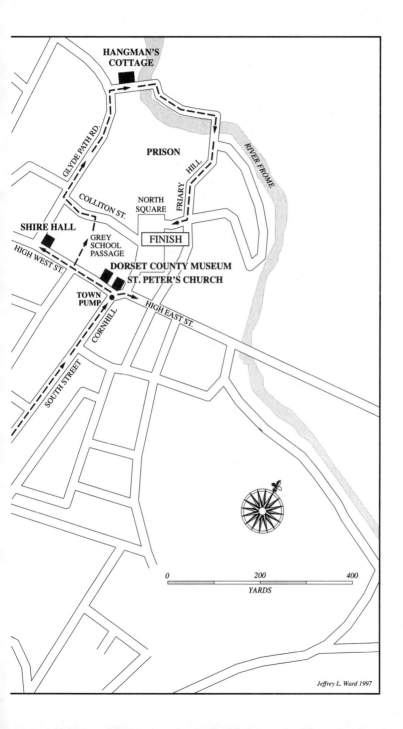

HANGMAN'S
COTTAGE

GLYDE PATH RD.

PRISON

RIVER FROME

COLLITON ST.

NORTH
SQUARE

FRIARY HILL

SHIRE HALL

GREY
SCHOOL
PASSAGE

FINISH

HIGH WEST ST.

DORSET COUNTY MUSEUM
ST. PETER'S CHURCH

TOWN
PUMP

CORNHILL

HIGH EAST ST.

SOUTH STREET

0   200   400
YARDS

Jeffrey L. Ward 1997

of Casterbridge: "Casterbridge" was Hardy's code for "Dorchester," "caster" and "chester" being two derivatives of the Roman word for military camp—*"castra."* (You will see dramatic evidence of the Romans' presence in the area.) Hardy, in childhood, had watched the hanging at Dorchester of a beautiful young woman who had murdered her oppressive husband. Hanging became a passionate interest of the novelist: his finest heroine, "Tess of the D'Urbervilles," ends on the gallows for a similar crime. Wasted sexuality, tragic landscapes; Hardy has made sure that for us the beauty of this place is haunted.

The walk will start at a **prehistoric earthwork,** used by the Romans. The route will then explore the town and its riverbank. Finally there is an excursion to a superb, dramatic, and lonely place dominating the Dorset countryside: the Iron-Age Celtic fortress now known as **Maiden Castle.**

Dorchester is reached by direct train from London's Waterloo station. (The journey takes less than two hours.) "**Dorchester South**" is the station where you arrive. The walk begins there. Cross the station forecourt, heading for the main road (**Weymouth Avenue**), and turn left onto its sidewalk. Walk uphill for about one hundred yards, then go through the gate on the left, into a field containing a steep grassy bank. This is **Maumbury Rings.** The entrance to the earthwork is a few yards ahead of you. Go to the entrance, or climb the rampart to its summit. You will see that the steep banks form a near-circle.

Maumbury Rings, according to archaeologists, began as a neolithic burial site: a date around 2500 B.C. has been estimated. Excavation has revealed that many shafts were dug into the earth here, and red deer skulls were buried in them. The site was taken over by Romans, who reshaped the banks and lowered the "floor" to make an amphitheater for games. Further changes to the banks were made in 1642, to create an artillery position from which, during the civil war, soldiers of parliament could ward off attacks on the town by the forces of Charles I.

The king's men did take Dorchester for a time. But the town had a Puritan tradition—in 1630 a shipful of Puritan families from Dorchester and area had sailed from Plymouth to America. There is also a record of a puppet show being banned in Dorchester out of Puritan high-mindedness. So there would have been much satisfaction here when the Royalist forces were ejected in 1644.

Maumbury Rings was the site of Dorchester's gallows in the eighteenth century. No doubt the banks made a good vantage point for spectators. Also, the edge-of-town site prevented complaints from neighbors; the behavior of hanging crowds was noisy and tasteless. Hardy wrote of this place: "Melancholy, impressive, lonely, yet accessible from every part of the town, the historic circle was the frequent spot for appointments of a furtive kind. Intrigues were arranged there; tentative meetings were there experimented after divisions and feuds." With its history of romance and death in a beautiful setting, Maumbury Rings was a place after Hardy's heart.

Retrace your steps through the gate into Weymouth Avenue: turn right, going downhill past the mighty brewery. Where six roads meet, take the third exit (almost straight ahead of you): **South Street.** A few yards into South Street, on the right, is a handsome stone **almshouse** of 1616, known at first as Napier's Mite, now as **Napper's Mite.** Another one hundred yards along South Street, on the right, is a fine Georgian **town house,** now used as a bank. This is believed to have been the inspiration in Thomas Hardy's mind, of Mayor Henchard's grand residence, before his fall.

South Street becomes **Cornhill:** walk toward its end. On the left notice the tall, graceful bay windows of the **Antelope,** in the eighteenth century a successful coaching inn, now a pleasant shopping precinct. The central passage between the bays was once the entry for carriages. Notice how the pilasters—flat, inset columns—at the front emphasize both the roundness and the height of the bay windows.

About ten yards from the end of Cornhill, a stone **obelisk** stands in the middle of the street. This was the town pump, built in 1784. Turn right for a moment into **High East Street** for a look at the **King's Arms Hotel** (and restaurant). This too was once an important coaching inn. Its bay window projects more proudly, less gracefully, than the Antelope's, over a columned porch. To the left of the porch is an arch where the carriages entered. Notice the spiked iron gate and the short iron posts on each side of the entrance, to protect the brickwork from battering by carriage wheels. Go to the porch and step inside to look at the elegant public rooms on the ground floor. In a corridor on the right, just past the reception desk, are atmospheric photographs of the area as Hardy knew it.

Back in High East Street, turn right and walk a few yards uphill to **St. Peter's Church**—just beyond the junction with Cornhill. If the church is open, go in. Just right of the altar, behind the door in a wooden screen, hangs a plan of the building done by Hardy, aged sixteen, when he was training here for his original profession of architect.

A few yards farther up the hill, on the same side of the road, is the **Dorset County Museum.** Look in for two things. The first is a small part of a skeleton, found in the 1930s when the hill fort of Maiden Castle was excavated. Between two vertebrae is lodged the head of a ballista-bolt—like a large arrow head. The ballista was a Roman weapon akin to a crossbow. Here, perhaps, we trace the death of a British defender of the fort, under attack from the invading legion of the general (later emperor) Vespasian, in A.D. 43–44. The other great treasure of the museum is its reconstruction of Thomas Hardy's study.

About twenty yards farther up the hill, on the opposite side of the street, is a handsome, timber-framed building from the early seventeenth century. It is now a pleasant restaurant and tea shop. In the 1680s its reputation in the town was not quite so innocent. Here lodged the infamous Judge Jeffreys, sent by the new and insecure Catholic king, James II, to punish Protestant rebels. The Protestants, led by the Duke of Monmouth (illegitimate son of the former king, Charles II), had fought here in the southwest in 1685 to overthrow King James. They lost. Monmouth himself was executed in London. Jeffreys toured the southwest sentencing Monmouth's followers in large numbers to be hung, drawn (disembowelled alive), and quartered. One advantage of this process was that it generated the maximum number of bloody bits to be publicly displayed in different places as a warning to other potential opponents. Such was the revulsion caused by Jeffreys's activities that when, three years later, a second Protestant army took the field, it chose the southwest as its point of departure, and won. James II crept out of his kingdom and fled to France. Jeffreys died in prison.

For another somber story, with a happier ending, come back across the street and go a few yards farther up the hill to **Shire Hall,** a fine if rather stark Georgian building from the 1790s. Here in 1834, six farm laborers were sentenced to be transported to Australia for seven years of penal servitude. Few returned from such punishment. At the time rural poverty in Dorset was intense. The men's crime had been to create, in the village of Tolpuddle, a labor union which involved secret oaths. At his trial, their leader George Loveless, said, "We have injured no man's reputation, character, person, or property. We were uniting to preserve ourselves, our wives, and our children from utter degradation and starvation." A public outcry greeted the sentences. In 1836 a pardon was issued, and by 1839 all the men had returned from the world's end. As the "Tolpuddle Martyrs" they became heroes of the labor movement. Here in the Shire Hall, the Crown Court (for serious criminal cases) is preserved in its Georgian form as a memorial to the men once condemned here. Check to see whether you may enter.

Go back a few yards down the hill and turn left into **Grey School Passage.** On the left you will see old, timbered cottages and on the right delightful cottage gardens adjoining a churchyard. Pass the ruin of a school building on the left. Where the street ends, turn left (into **Colliton Street**) and after one hundred yards, go right into **Glyde Path Road,** noting the superb, weathered stone of a grand Georgian building across the road. As you walk downhill on Glyde Path Road there are more pretty cottages on the right, this time with wooden canopies at their doors. Just before the road bends left, there is a fine cottage of mellow, red brick on the left. Look for the ghost of a former doorway, now bricked up, revealing that in less prosperous times, this was once two cottages rather than one.

Follow the bend of the road. Twenty yards beyond it, turn sharp right and go down a few yards to the thatched cottage which stands by the **River Frome** (pronounced "Froom"). All is elegant and wholesome. The thatch is trim; the rest of the structure is well maintained and burglar-alarmed. The name is proudly painted twice: **"Hangman's Cottage."** Here, in bygone days of rural squalor, lived the local executioner, discreetly tucked away on the edge of town, as befitted his repellent work. His noose, it is said, was kept hidden under the thatch. The cottage symbolizes the new prosperity of the English countryside, or at least of its prettiest parts. Until the 1960s, life here would have been far plainer.

Pass the cottage and cross a bridge to a lovely spot for country children. An overflow of the River Frome makes a little pool, controlled by a wooden hatch. Here under the trees, in spring, we found children netting baby trout and showing them proudly to passersby.

Turn right and walk along the bank of the Frome, an idyllic walk on the edge of the fields. Across the river and to the right you will glimpse the high, arched window of a red brick Victorian building. This was, and is, **Dorchester Prison.** Hardy would have found it grimly satisfying that there is still a serpent in this rural Eden.

Cross the first bridge and go up **Friary Hill,** which becomes **North Square.** Go over, on the left, to the late-Georgian building of red brick named, on a stone plaque outside, **Chubb's Alms House** (1822). Look at the massive, antique door, which has Victorian Gothic arches set into its wood. Continue along North Square until it emerges at a spot you will recognize—opposite the town pump in Cornhill.

After your exploration of the town, you have earned a break. Perhaps have a meal at one of the ancient hostelries which we noted earlier—they are all within a few yards. Afterward, if you are energetic, there is a walk you will long remember, around Maiden Castle.

Maiden Castle is approached by the road on which you began the last walk, Weymouth Avenue—the main route past Maumbury Rings. (So, after visiting Maiden Castle, you can return to Dorchester South railway station without re-entering the town.) Shortly after passing the Rings you bear off to the right, along **Maiden Castle Lane.** The walk from the center of town to the castle and back to the station is about four miles. You will also want to take time exploring the mighty ramparts of the castle. A good compromise might be to take a taxi to the castle, and to walk back.

Maiden Castle is an earthwork vastly bigger than Maumbury Rings. Its ramparts enclose about forty-seven acres. Archaeologists estimate that it was begun about 500 B.C., in other words long before the Romans were a cloud on the horizon of Celtic northern Europe. For the local Celts, the enemy was presumably—other Celts. Even today, after millennia of erosion, the grassy ramparts, and the ditches between them, are so deep that when standing among them, you can feel cut off from the world. Hill forts of this design were the centers of Celtic power in the Iron Age, the last few centuries before the Roman conquest. The element *-den,* in the name "Maiden," is found in various forms across the formerly Celtic world; Lyon in France was Lug*dun*um, the Netherlands has Lei*den,* Scotland has *Dun*dee, near Dublin is *Dun* Laoghaire. Even Lon*don* was probably another such name. And in Welsh, the only thriving Celtic language left in Britain, the word for "city" is still *dinas.* Within a *dun,* cattle and sheep, prime objects of Celtic wealth, could be sheltered from enemies. Such is the size of Maiden that there might even be worthwhile grazing between the ramparts.

In this sleeping earthwork, remote from cities, you may find that you have the place almost to yourself. Walk around the whole perimeter of the outer rampart, for matchless views over the empty countryside of Dorset. Or perhaps, in sunshine, lie with your back on a rampart and gaze at a view made only of grass and sky.

Phone: Tourist Information, Dorchester: 01305 267992

HAY-ON-WYE ✦

Hay-on-Wye is a small town on the border of Wales, with narrow, twisting streets of old houses, dominated by the homely ruin of a castle overlooking the vale of the River Wye. The course of the river is rocky, broken, and dramatic. The walks along its banks are famous, but never crowded. The village streets are more for walkers than for cars. And many of the walkers have come for a day's holiday, to find two things: atmosphere and books.

Hay has a mass of secondhand bookstores. It's claimed that between them the stores hold the largest collection in the world. The stores specialize: this one in history, that one in children's books, another in novels. . . . If there's a book you've long hoped to find, American or British, this is the place to try.

People who come for books stay for other things. Craftworkers flourish here. So do antique stores, unspoilt pubs, teashops. Businesses change, but still we've given some details. Even though this or that business may not last, the details are still a good guide to the feel of the town.

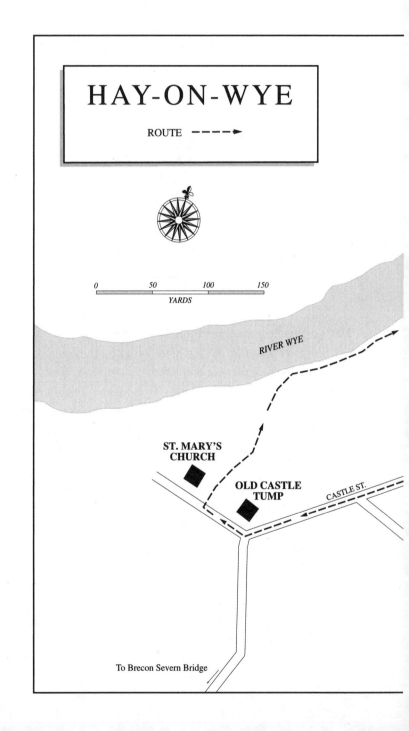

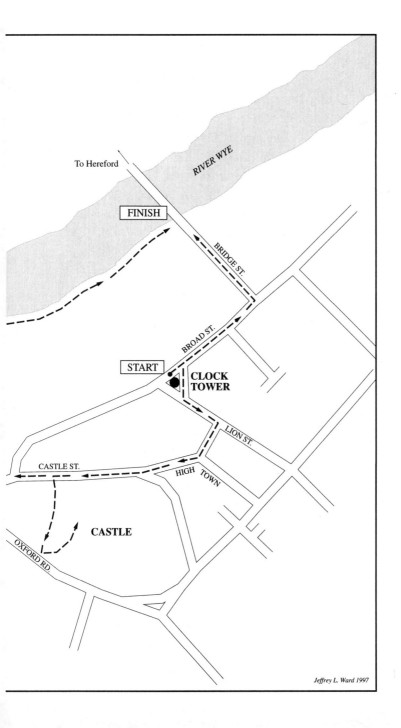

Because it's a border town, just inside Wales, local feelings vary over whether the place is "really" Welsh or English. The castle was built by the English to control the Welsh. The Welsh duly attacked it. Now it's the English who may feel they are being dominated. Some complain at the fact that their children, from the age of five, have to learn the Welsh language in school. One local solution has been the good-humored campaign to declare "Home rule for Hay!" (Independence was declared on April Fool's Day, 1977.) Look out for oval stickers on the rear of cars declaring the vehicle's "nationality": not "G.B." but "Hay." The idea of home rule was the brainchild of Richard Booth, a man of vision. It is he who, since 1961, has made Hay a place of books; in his words, "its very remoteness protecting its trade from domination by London." The inhabitable parts of the castle have been Booth's home. Local people sometimes call him—with a twinkle—the "King of Hay."

The remoteness of Hay means that, if you come by public transport, you will need ingenuity. The nearest railway station is Hereford, about twenty miles away. From Hereford to Hay there are some five buses each weekday. For details of transport, probably the best first step is to call the Tourist Information at Hay. Its number is given below. Don't let the distance put you off. It's the remoteness that makes Hay a happy and successful place. The people who come are those who really want to be here!

Start your walk in the center of the town at the **clock tower,** with its pointed arches in Victorian gothic style. A few feet from the base of the clock tower is an old metal post bearing the sign "Brecon County." (Brecon has since been abolished as a county. Hay is now in the Welsh supercounty of Powys.) From the clock tower, walk some thirty yards along **Broad Street** to the former granary on the right, now a tearoom. Above its door is the opening from which bags of flour were once hoisted. Walk another twenty-five yards along Broad Street until you see, on the opposite, left, side, a lawyer's office marked "Williams, Beales & Co., Solicitors." Now look, on your own side of the street and very close to you, for another lawyer's office, with the name "Gabb & Co"—a name which Dickens might have found appropriate for the legal profession, which he loved to satirize. In the 1920s, when there were different sets of lawyers in these same offices, rivalry between the two led to tragedy and a national scandal.

In the office where "Williams, Beales" now are, worked the solicitor Major Henry Armstrong. His business was failing, and he could look across the street to the rival firm opposite, which was doing much better. Lack of money was producing tensions in the Armstrong household. Local men and women in Hay still agree that Armstrong's wife was oppressive. It is said that when her husband had tipped the porter at the railway station, his wife would go and reclaim the money. Armstrong poisoned her with arsenic. ("She's buried in Cusop churchyard," a local man told us, "but there's no gravestone!" Armstrong evidently had more pressing calls on his money.) Fortified by his apparent success in disposing of his wife, Armstrong made plans for his business rival across the street. The lawyer in question became suspicious when Armstrong, out of character, kept urging gifts of food on him. Eventually he took some, had it analyzed, and found that it was poisoned. Mrs. Armstrong's body was exhumed and found to contain similar poison. The luckless Major Armstrong was tried and hung. He is remembered in Hay with some sympathy. One local informant, male, told us Armstrong had a poor defense attorney. Another, female, reported that a present-day lawyer in Armstrong's former offices claims to think that the Major was innocent. "But," she said, "nobody else does."

Thirty yards farther along Broad Street is the Poetry Bookshop; its sign advertises specialties also in "Children's, mysticism, mythology, and women's studies." Farther along Broad Street lies the

Dulas Brook, the frontier with England. But cross now to the pub **The Three Tuns,** on the corner with **Bridge Street.**

The Three Tuns, with its uneven frontage and chimneys, is well known in Hay as an earthy, endearing place. (A tun, by the way, was a huge wooden barrel.) At the time of writing, its interior suggests the way very many early twentieth-century British pubs reflected the personality of the landlady or landlord. Later in the century, breweries caused the pubs to be stereotyped, their bars redesigned at the command of accountants. Go in, or look through the low window at the tiled floor and at the ceiling tinted by tobacco. Turn into Bridge Street. At the side of the Three Tuns are stone **mounting steps**—for customers in the nineteenth century who, after drinking, needed help in reaching the saddle.

As you go along Bridge Street, the first house on the right has a fine stone canopy and a pleasant arrangement of metal in the glass above the door. These features date from about 1800. Note the antique bellpull, inset to the right of the door.

A few yards farther, just before the bridge, a pathway to the right leads down to a delightful picnic area and to riverside walks. (Our own riverside walk comes at the end of the chapter. It may lead you back to this spot.) Walk onto the (modern) bridge, then look back for a fine view of the town, with the clock tower and the castle on the skyline.

Now, to explore the rest of the town, walk back to the clock tower. On reaching it, turn left from Broad Street uphill into **Lion Street.** Passing the fine façade of a bookshop on the left, take the first right and look for the entrance to the business of "The Hay Makers." In the courtyard here are sold handsome leather-bound notebooks made locally. There are wooden platters, engraved to order. When we visited, the carver was at work designing an engraving in ancient Greek for a customer.

A few yards uphill from the Hay Makers you will notice, on the left, the stone columns of the former **Butter Market,** an elegant, single-storied, Georgian building. Go closer and see, above its main gate, the name and date of the builder, carved in stone: "W. Enoch, 1833." Next door, up the hill, is another stylish building from the early nineteenth century, the **Town Hall,** of 1840. Its first story is, like the Butter Market, open to the winds. This was a cheese market.

Walk uphill, with the Town Hall on your left. Where the building ends, a view of the **Castle** opens up, to the left. First are the towering ruins of the medieval section, attacked in 1402 by the forces of the charismatic Welshman Owain Glyndwr—"Glendower" in Shakespeare. His brief, promising campaign for the independence of his country ended in his own disappearance. (He is still revered in Wales, the lost leader. Some young Welsh independence-seekers of the 1980s, pursued by the English authorities, named themselves "Meibion Glyndwr"—"Glyndwr's boys.") In the tall trees, at the near end of the castle wall, you may hear the chattering of jackdaws. For them the crevices in the old walls make ideal nesting sites.

Running uphill before you, parallel with the castle walls, is **Castle Street.** Walk on its left side until you come to a hefty wooden door, studded with iron and set in a long stone wall. This is the entrance to the **Honesty Bookshop,** an open air display of inexpensive books. There's no attendant. It's up to you to leave the required small coins for whatever you take. If the door is open, go in. This is a good spot to view the inhabited part of the castle, high above you. It was built in the early 1600s. The long windows gave a view over Wales, just in case. But rebellion was no longer likely, and a gentler style of architecture was used on the building's far side, facing England: you'll see it shortly.

Continue up Castle Street for about forty yards, then turn left into the alley called **Back Fold.** Follow the alley as it winds to the right. Where it reaches a road, turn sharp left (following the signs to Booth's Books) and you will find yourself in the outbuildings of the castle. You're now in a cobbled yard, amid cottage architecture and low stone roofs covered in moss. A bookshop here specializes in works on Native Americans and on cinema. To see the front of the castle, and its magnificent lawn, go back a few yards and, where the buildings end, turn left and look over the stone wall. Above the main façade of the castle are three elegant gables, in the Jacobean style of Shakespeare's era.

Retrace your steps toward Back Fold. Thirty yards from the castle, when you reach the road and before you make the sharp turn again into the alley, look across the road to the modern single-storied building which houses the Craft Center. Here local artists in jewelry, glass, leather, and wood sell their work. Return down Back Fold. When you reach Castle Street once more, turn left and walk forty yards. Here, on the left of the street, uneven stone steps lead up to the small, intriguing shop of Ms. Athene English. The shop has a sideline in old-fashioned, but working, fishing tackle, of the style long used on trout and salmon rivers like the Wye. Rods of split cane and fishing baskets ("creels") of wicker are the favorites. But the glory of the shop, and Ms. English's own craft, is leather. Among the purses, wallets, and organizers are some, made by English, from eighteenth-century reindeer hides. The hides were Russian, destined for Italy but involved in a shipwreck off the British coast, where a few years ago they were recovered by divers, treated and, thanks to the sea water, found to be in good order after two hundred years.

From English's shop go fifty yards farther along Castle Street to the corner with the Blue Boar pub. Then, farther on the left of Castle Street, look at the first house beyond the pub, with the former stable building beside it and a stone arch leading into the old stable yard. The next building on the left is the former town cinema, now an enormous bookshop. Thirty yards farther, on the right of the street, is the most comfortable hotel in the town, "The Swan at Hay." Immediately before the hotel, turn right into the lane which is signed as leading to St. Mary's church. Twenty-five yards along the lane, on the left, look into the yard of the Swan hotel. This was designed for horses and carriages. You'll see the former stables.

Back in the lane, fifty yards farther on the right is a field with a fine earthwork. It's perhaps twenty feet high and thirty yards across, with well-preserved grassy ramparts running around it. At this spot, two elderly local gentlemen gave us detailed and accurate information about the area. But asked about the earthwork one said, "Oh we don't know what that is. We call it the "Tumpy Field." "Tump" means "mound," in the language of the border counties. This tump in reality was an early medieval castle, with "motte and bailey" (mound and wooden stockade). Just after the tump, and before the church, turn right, off the road, and follow the wooden signpost marked to the "Waterfall and Warren." The waterfall is tiny, part of a stream. But in about one hundred yards the path brings you to the bank of the Wye. Turn right and the riverside walk will bring you back to the bridge where you began the tour.

Useful phone numbers:
Tourist Information office, Hay: 01497 820144
The Swan at Hay Hotel, 01497 821188

✤ KNOLE

Knole is the one great country house among our walks. Henry VIII was an early resident, and part of the building was made to his designs. So large and complex are the house and its outbuildings that they have been likened to a medieval village. Yet the place sits discreetly on its hilltop (its knoll—whence the name), well screened by tall trees, and only by exploring in its grounds do you find viewpoints to show how expansive the house is. The grounds themselves are a delight. They extend over one thousand acres and are open to the public. House and grounds belong to the National Trust. Lord Sackville, whose ancestor was given the place by Elizabeth I, still lives in part of the building. Visitors see the more impressive of the rooms and walk in the main courtyards.

For many visitors the most enjoyable aspects of Knole are the great walls of the mansion, with their **battlements,** and the broad **parklands** with their herds of deer and ancient trees. There are also some treasures of painting and metalwork within, as you will see. For connoisseurs of old furniture Knole is unique. In the late seventeenth century the (scandalous) sixth earl of Sackville used his position in charge of royal palaces to amass countless furnishings of almost unimaginable splendor and value. These are now treated as Knole's chief claim to attention. However, the colors of the fabric have faded severely over the centuries. The celebrated furniture is, in many cases, unexciting to the untrained eye. And, to reduce further fading, some of the display rooms are kept deliberately half-lit. So we suggest that you resist the pressure to see Knole mainly as a museum of furniture. Choose a few objects on which to concentrate—always a good plan, in any case, for reducing "museum fatigue." Our comments guide you toward the more lively and human aspects of the history of Knole.

Knole is open only from April to October. On Wednesdays, Fridays–Sundays, the hours are 11:00–5:00; Thursdays 2:00–5:00. Knole is on the outskirts of the town of **Sevenoaks.** Trains from London (Charing Cross station) to Sevenoaks take about half-an-hour. Knole is therefore popular with Londoners. We suggest that, if possible, you visit on a weekday.

From Sevenoaks railway station to the entrance of **Knole Park** is about a mile. But the walk is up a long, steep hill, in colorless suburban surroundings. Take a taxi, if you can, and do your walking in the countryside around the great house.

Begin your stroll as you enter the park between a pair of small Georgian **gatehouses.** You are now descending the side of a small valley. Near the valley floor, as the motor road bears left, bear right on a footpath uphill. The scattered trees, many of them very old and easily penetrated, are ideal for woodpeckers. We saw two species, including the large Green Woodpecker, usually detected by its loud, laughing cry. You may also see deer in this valley.

As you climb out of the valley you see the grand façade of **Knole House.** Your eye may fall first on the curved gables. These were the fashion in the reign of James I. Probably they were added by

Thomas Sackville, first earl of Dorset, shortly after 1600. Much of the house had been built in the late fifteenth century—to the order of an Archbishop of Canterbury, Thomas Bourchier. Like most church property, it was seized in the days of Henry VIII. The Archbishop who lived here in Henry's day, Cranmer, was understandably reluctant to let it go. His secretary described how Cranmer was "minded to have retained Knole unto himself." He tried in vain to deflect the king, claiming that Knole was too small for the royal requirements. Henry bluffly replied, "Marry, I had rather have it than this house [Otford] . . . it standeth on a sound, perfect and wholesome ground; and if I should make abode here, as I do surely mind to do *now and then*. . . ." So the king got it. It is thought that the **great gatehouse,** through which you will shortly enter, was made to Henry's order. Its four turrets at each corner, with battlements, recall the gatehouse Henry built at St. James's Palace in London. Other grandees of the sixteenth century who stayed at Knole were Henry's Catholic daughter, the future Queen Mary I, and the hated John Dudley, whose schemes to supplant Mary brought Protestant Jane Grey to the throne for nine days, and then—with Dudley himself—to the scaffold.

Before you enter, first stand back from the gatehouse and look up for the heraldic leopard which is the motif of the Sackville family. Then, just outside the door and a foot or two to the left, look for the discreet doorbells of private residents. You will probably see the names "Sackville"—and also "Sackville-West." The latter name will be familiar to those who know the Bloomsbury Group. Vita Sackville-West, one of the family, is famous for her tempestuous and well-documented times with her lover Violet Trefusis. She also wrote a history of Knole, parts of which you can find reprinted in the inexpensive and very useful National Trust guidebook to Knole, sold at the door here.

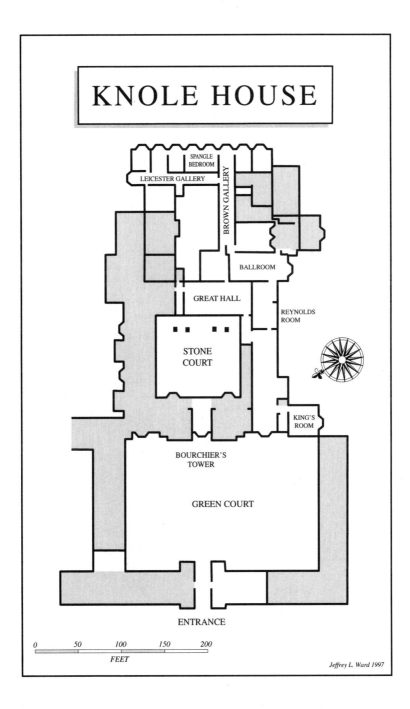

KNOLE HOUSE

SPANGLE BEDROOM

LEICESTER GALLERY

BROWN GALLERY

BALLROOM

GREAT HALL

REYNOLDS ROOM

STONE COURT

KING'S ROOM

BOURCHIER'S TOWER

GREEN COURT

ENTRANCE

0   50   100   150   200

FEET

Jeffrey L. Ward 1997

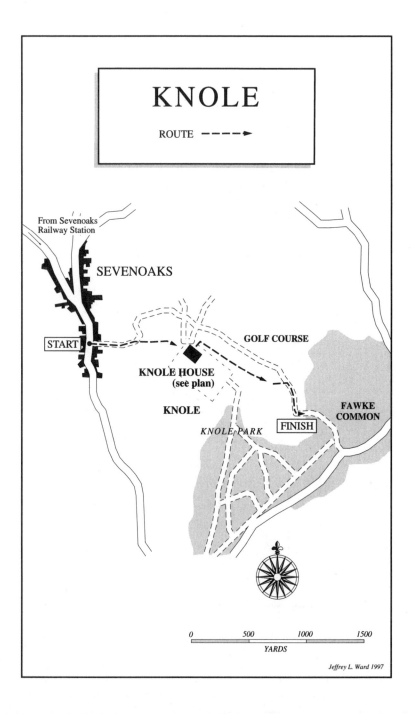

Once through the door (admission charge) you are in the **Green Court,** with its broad lawns, the largest of seven courtyards at Knole. The large number of small windows is taken as evidence that much of this first court was built to accommodate the numerous servants of Henry VIII. Directly opposite the outer gatehouse, through which you have just come, stands another gatehouse. This was the one built almost a century before Henry's time by Archbishop Bourchier, before the Green Court was added. Above the arched entrance to Bourchier's gatehouse is a projecting—"**oriel**"—**window.** Level with the top of the window, on each side, are three small arched recesses. These are **machicolations,** whether real or ornamental: through such grooves boiling oil or molten lead was poured upon attackers.

Go through the archway into **Stone Court.** Great flagstones pave the court. Below them are cisterns in which was stored drinking water, channeled here from the gutters of the house. The curved gables above the court, and the Doric colonnade at its side, were made to Thomas Sackville's order in the reign of James I. So were the handsome, and deliberately varied, **lead drainpipes** which have the date 1605 molded at their head. Cross the court and look back toward **Bourchier's gatehouse.** The tower to the right of the gatehouse is known as **Shelley's Tower.** "Shelley" here is a corruption of an Italian name: Giannetta Baccelli had rooms in the tower in the late eighteenth century. She was the mistress of John Frederick Sackville, the third duke of Dorset, and had been a famous dancer. You will see something of this striking lady in a moment.

From Stone Court go into the **Great Hall.** Highly ornate paneling from the seventeenth century stands high at one end. In a gallery behind its upper section an orchestra used to play. At each side of the wide fireplace is a link, a portable oil lamp, surmounted with a crown of the style favored by the Stuart dynasty. In the fireplace itself, firedogs bear the initials "H" and "A." These stood for Henry VIII and Anne Boleyn, and were brought here in the nineteenth century from the Boleyn family home at Hever Castle. At the end of the hall opposite to the orchestra look at the portrait of the first earl who reshaped so much of the house, as well as put the oak screen and paneling into this hall.

From the Great Hall, turn left to the foot of the **Great Staircase.** Here are memorials to the beauty of Giannetta Baccelli. In the lobby at the foot of the staircase is a sketch showing the society portraitist, Thomas Gainsborough, engaged in painting Miss Baccelli. (That painting is now in London, at the Tate Gallery.) Much more striking here, is the full-size sculpture, in plaster, of Baccelli. She is shown on a sofa, lying naked and provocative on her front and displaying what for the third duke, her patron, was perhaps the finest indoor view at Knole.

Go up the staircase. Here the museum of furniture begins. The long **Brown Gallery,** with its superb oak paneling, has very many portraits from the sixteenth and seventeenth centuries. Beyond, the **Spangle Bedroom** has a handsome four-poster bed, which once glittered with spangles (sequins). The paintings in this room were acquired by the energetic sixth earl. As the guide book says with polite restraint, the pictures "mostly represent ladies he must have known at the court of Charles II." There were many such ladies. One portrait here is of a "wild oat": Lady Shannon, the sixth earl's natural daughter.

The sixth earl, the accumulator of the furnishings around you, was a major figure in the politics and high society of late seventeenth-century England. He was a trusted crony of Charles II. When Charles made the Secret Treaty of Dover in 1670, giving the French king a promise to reconvert England to Catholicism in return for French cash to support Charles's lifestyle, the sixth earl was sent to France to be the ambassador who would keep matters smooth and secret. (If news had leaked of the Treaty, England very likely would have been plunged once again into civil war.) In his earlier days, the young Sackville had kept Nell Gwynne as his mistress—before Charles II did. Since Sackville's name was also Charles, Nell Gwynne is supposed to have described him as "My Charles the First." Samuel Pepys in his diary describes how, in 1668, young Sackville had been beaten and imprisoned for various nocturnal capers.

In the **Billiard Room** are billiard cues with ivory tips, from the time of Charles I. Look into the **Venetian Ambassador's Room** for a highly ornate bed, brought by the sixth earl from the royal palace of Whitehall. The bed was made for King James II in 1688. Judging by its ornate carving and sumptuous fabric, it may have been for the king's own use. The king cannot have slept easy in it for long. Later in that year he was ejected from Britain in favor of a Protestant ruler.

Look now, at the end of the **Leicester Gallery,** for the fine china delightfully displayed in Lady Betty Germain's china closet. China preserves its colors better than fabric. Then go back along the Brown Gallery to the door at its end (on the left), and enter the Ballroom. This was originally built in the 1460s to be Archbishop Bourchier's main living room. The hugely elaborate carving—look especially at the chimneypiece—was added in the early seventeenth century.

In the **Reynolds Room,** so called because many of the large paintings are by Sir Joshua Reynolds, look especially for the artist's portraits of the poet Oliver Goldsmith and of Dr. Johnson. Look up to see the Sackville leopard molded in the ceiling.

Go on to the **Cartoon Gallery** to look at the gilt table and candlestands. These were probably given as diplomatic sweeteners to the sixth earl by the French king, Louis XIV, when the earl was ambassador, in the aftermath of the delicate Secret Treaty.

The **King's Room,** reputedly where James I once stayed, has furnishings overwhelmingly expensive in their day. Silver on the wall was meant to reflect candlelight. The towering four-poster bed is a rare survivor from the age of Louis XIV. The atmosphere in the room is of darkly oppressive luxury.

In the **King's Closet** nearby look for the small chest in crimson velvet near the door. This was a closestool—a portable toilet— probably found by the sixth earl in a royal palace and brought to Knole. (An earlier Sackville, similarly acquisitive of wealth, was nicknamed—by a play on his name—"Fillsack.") From the far end of the Cartoon Gallery a staircase will bring you down to Stone Court. From here go back through Green Court and out through the main entrance.

Once outside the House, turn right and, where the house ends, right again. On the right, in the former **stable area,** you will find a welcome café and rest rooms.

For a walk in the grounds, come out of the café and turn right. Your path will run parallel to the wall of the House and its gardens. As the path goes uphill it runs, as a narrow road, between a lovely avenue of tall trees. Where the garden wall runs off at a right angle to the right, go straight ahead and pass, on your left, a lodge with gothic windows and near-conical towers. You now cross part of a **golf course.** A choice of walks lies in your view. Downhill to the left, past a small pond, you can walk toward a long wood. Or, in the opposite direction and slightly uphill, is a walk heading for the sky-line between rows of tall trees.

Phone: Knole House 01732 450608

OXFORD I ⚜

Oxford with its ancient colleges is incomparable. The college towers, "quads" (quadrangles), cloisters, chapels, halls, and gardens will delight you. The yellow stone of the old buildings gives a warmth and friendliness to the place.

The main streets of Oxford are crowded. The many lanes and back alleys are quieter, though an undergraduate on a rickety bicycle or a small party of visitors may always be around the next corner. The chief beauties of the colleges are hidden. Only by going down passageways and peering into colleges will you find the places which the true Oxonians most enjoy.

In recent years access to the college grounds has become less predictable. At exam times (April–June), when many of the students are under stress, and at the high season for visitors, several colleges are off limits for part of the time. Our walks have been designed to avoid this problem as far as possible.

Even on a short visit you will see signs of the mental character of Oxford life. Only since the 1970s have the colleges been coed.

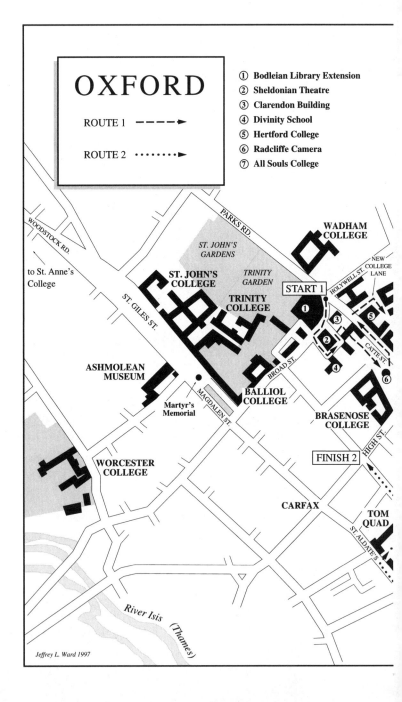

OXFORD

ROUTE 1 ----▶

ROUTE 2 ·······▶

① Bodleian Library Extension
② Sheldonian Theatre
③ Clarendon Building
④ Divinity School
⑤ Hertford College
⑥ Radcliffe Camera
⑦ All Souls College

WOODSTOCK RD.

PARKS RD.

WADHAM COLLEGE

ST. JOHN'S GARDENS

NEW COLLEGE LANE

HOLYWELL ST.

to St. Anne's College

ST. JOHN'S COLLEGE

TRINITY GARDEN

START 1

TRINITY COLLEGE

ST. GILES ST.

① ③ ⑤

② CATTE ST.

ASHMOLEAN MUSEUM

BROAD ST.

④

⑥

Martyr's Memorial

MAGDALEN ST.

BALLIOL COLLEGE

BRASENOSE COLLEGE

HIGH ST.

WORCESTER COLLEGE

FINISH 2

CARFAX

TOM QUAD

ST. ALDATE'S

River Isis (Thames)

Jeffrey L. Ward 1997

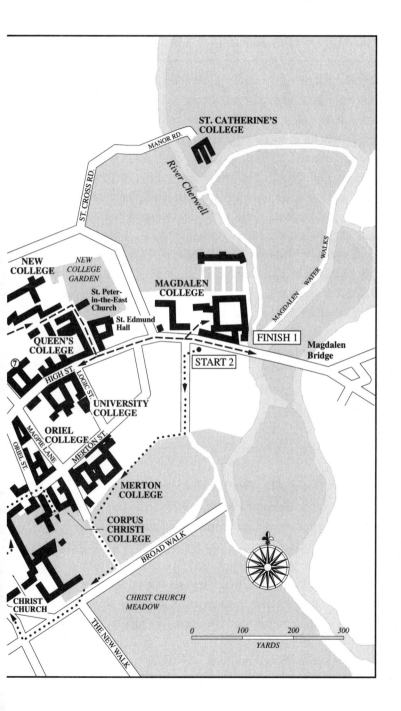

ST. CATHERINE'S
COLLEGE

MANOR RD.

River Cherwell

ST. CROSS RD.

MAGDALEN WATER WALKS

NEW
COLLEGE

NEW
COLLEGE
GARDEN

St. Peter-
in-the-East
Church

MAGDALEN
COLLEGE

St. Edmund
Hall

QUEEN'S
COLLEGE

FINISH 1

Magdalen
Bridge

⑦

HIGH ST.

LOGIC ST.

START 2

UNIVERSITY
COLLEGE

ORIEL
COLLEGE

MAGPIE LANE

ORIEL ST.

MERTON ST.

MERTON
COLLEGE

CORPUS
CHRISTI
COLLEGE

BROAD WALK

CHRIST
CHURCH

CHRIST CHURCH
MEADOW

THE NEW WALK

0   100   200   300

YARDS

Antique spikes crown many college walls, designed to thwart the wilder male undergraduates who wished to return from their girlfriends after the gates were locked. The older "dons" (university teachers) grew up in single-sex institutions with a monastic atmosphere. Some are still ill at ease in female company.

In spite of colorful student rebellions from time to time, the political tone is relaxed and conservative. Most of the students attended private schools. British prime ministers tend to come from Oxford, and there is among the students more high ambition than high principle. Oxford shows more of a sense of humor than Cambridge, where political ideals and intellectual fashions are taken more seriously. Even in the late 1960s, when students were changing the world and passionate graffiti were everywhere, the walls of Oxford carried more risqué or witty messages. There was a national strike of seamen: so a graffito here ran "Save our seamen—Oxford's new emissions policy." Another wall carried a political maxim about political maxims: "Aphorism is the death-rattle of revolution."

Oxford is easily reached from London—either just over an hour by fast train from Paddington or about an hour and three-quarters by car from Hyde Park Corner. There are also good, inexpensive, and very frequent buses to Oxford, from Victoria coach station and Hyde Park Corner.

Start your stroll through England's Senior University in the center of the university, on **Broad Street** (or, as it's called in Oxford, "the Broad") at the corner of **Catte Street.** Though the colleges in effect comprise the university, this is the university's administrative headquarters.

Pause for a moment on "the Broad" by the weather-worn stone busts of the so-called **Roman emperors.** The style is slightly grotesque. Look at the emphasis on the teeth. The classic **Claren-**

don building on the corner was built by Nicholas Hawksmoor, a pupil of Christopher Wren.

Twenty yards before the corner, go up the steps and glance through the beautiful wrought iron gates under the archway with the university's motto: *Dominus illuminatio mea* ("My Enlightenment is the Lord"), to the series of Bodleian arches and the **Radcliffe Camera.** This circular building with a great dome and striking parapet, used as one of the Bodleian's main reading rooms, is a handsome eighteenth-century structure and one of Oxford's landmarks.

Go for a moment to the rounded Sheldonian Theatre, behind the emperor's heads, one of Oxford's architectural treasures. It was built in 1664–1669 to provide a place for university functions such as the awarding of degrees previously held in St. Mary's Church. Some of the ceremonies in the mid-seventeenth century had become too uproarious for a church, so Archbishop Sheldon provided the funds for a lay building.

Sir Christopher Wren designed the Sheldonian as a copy of the Theater of Marcellus in Rome. Have a look at the huge oak **south doors** at the back, on the side farthest from the emperors, which are opened for the academic processions.

The bright, impressive interior has been repainted in its original colors. Your eye will be drawn at once to the magnificent unsupported roof, one of Wren's remarkable engineering achievements. The painted ceiling is intended to suggest an open Roman theater. The vice-chancellor's chair stands in the center of the curved tiers of seats, and to its right you will see the beautifully carved rostrum. If the building is closed, a small gap between the great doors here will give you a glimpse of the interior.

As you stand facing, and next to, the great doors, turn ninety degrees right and walk to the arched entrance to a passage leading to the Old Schools. Walk along the passage. This early seventeenth-century quadrangle now houses the old part of the world-renowned **Bodleian Library,** named for Sir Thomas Bodley who refounded the university library in 1602 when he presented his great collection.

On your left is the **Tower of the Five Orders:** the various classic styles of architecture are, as the eye moves upward, Doric, Tuscan, Ionic, Corinthian, and Composite. Near the top is a statue of the monarch of the day, James I. Around you, various doorways bear the names of the Old Schools (lecture rooms), written in Latin in the university's colors of dark blue and gold. Among them are the former schools of astronomy, rhetoric, and metaphysics. On the side opposite the tower is the public entrance to the Bodleian library. Go in. From 10:30 on weekdays there are regular tours of the fifteenth-century **Duke Humfrey's Library** and exhibition room (open weekdays, 9:30–5:00). Superb illuminated manuscripts, antique folios, and early records are on display. The seventeenth-century shelves contain books still arranged in their original classification by size and subject (Theology, Medicine, Law, and Arts). The elaborate ceiling, decorated with the university arms, and huge oak beams, give the room an air in keeping with the library's distinction. Following Bodley's instructions, a bell is still rung at the closing of the library. Upstairs are reading rooms with decorative ceilings, painted panels, and quaint friezes.

Whether or not you take the tour, go through on the ground floor here to the **Divinity School,** below Duke Humfrey's Library. Built in fifteenth-century, Perpendicular Gothic style, this room with its superb **vaulted ceiling** and great bosses is of exceptional beauty and nobility. The west door of the Divinity School leads to **Convocation House** where the governing assemblies of the University meet and where Parliament gathered when the plague forced it to evacuate London during the mid-seventeenth century.

Back out in the quad by the tower, look right for the **Exhibition Room,** where treasures of the library are displayed in rotation.

Close to it go through the central archway—between the doors which say "*Schola musicae*" and "*Schola naturalis philosophiae*" to the adjacent Radcliffe Camera.

A few yards on your right as you face the entrance to the Radcliffe Camera is the massive gate tower to **Brasenose College,** known to Oxonians as B.N.C. Its odd name comes from the medieval brass doorknocker, in the shape of a lion's head, which is now kept in the college's dining hall, behind the High Table (the table where the dons sit). A dull copy, barely distinguishable, is now before you at the top of the college's main entrance door. If you go through the gate into the quad, look for the lovely painted sundial on the right. The dining hall, and the knocker, are on the left side of the quad.

Standing at the entrance to Brasenose, and looking in the direction of the Radcliffe Camera, you will see, behind the Radcliffe Camera, part of Oxford's most exclusive college, **All Souls.** There are no undergraduate students here. Nor is there much access for the public. To be a Fellow (i.e., a don) of All Souls is hailed even by other Oxonians as a mark of extreme academic brilliance. Skeptics, however, note that Fellows are appointed early in adult life. The appointment involves a prediction that much profound research will be published in the scholar's maturity—a prediction not always fulfilled.

Go across, passing on your left the Radcliffe Camera, to the black-and-gold iron gate, and look into a cloistered quad of All Souls. Straight ahead are twin towers by Hawksmoor. On the left of the quad is another lovely sundial.

With your back to the black-and-gold gate, and staying on the same sidewalk, walk to the right. This is Catte Street. From this street, about one hundred yards beyond the Radcliffe Camera, turn right into **New College Lane.** Almost immediately you pass under the arching **bridge of Hertford College,** Oxford's version of the

"Bridge of Sighs." Look for the lovely leaded windows of the bridge. Cross New College Lane. Five yards beyond the bridge, turn left into the alley. This twists to the right and reaches the **Turf tavern.** This fine, intimate spot is—for those who can find it—a favorite place for long, sleepy lunches in the summer. The tavern is hidden on all sides by the backs of tall buildings. The shelter of these buildings creates a sun-trap. As you approach the outdoor tables of the tavern, notice the iron standard of a former gaslamp, with the heraldic Ox of Oxford molded on its base.

Come back to New College Lane and turn left. The lane twists first right and then left. Altogether it is about two hundred yards from the Bridge of Sighs to the wooden gate at the entrance to New College (admission charge, when open).

The buildings and grounds of **New College,** founded by William of Wykeham in 1379, are among the most enchanting in Oxford. The original foundation was called St. Mary College of Winchester in Oxford and the name New College may have originated to distinguish it from the older "House of Blessed Mary the Virgin in Oxford," known as Oriel. New College was the first college established for the sole purpose of preparing undergraduates for the arts degree.

After passing through the entrance gate, turn sharply to the left in the front quad, then left again in the corner. In a moment you will be in the glorious **cloisters.** Here more than anywhere else in Oxford you will sense the contemplative spirit of the Middle Ages. Stroll for a few minutes under the wood vaulting of the fourteenth-century cloisters. As you pause by the venerable **ilex tree,** at the far edge of the velvetlike turf, look up at the crenellated **bell tower** above the weathered, gray stone roof of the cloister. This is indeed one of the most tranquil and timeless spots in Oxford.

New College Chapel is quite outstanding. The entrance is in the short passage you have already walked, between the cloisters and the quad. The ante-chapel contains windows of fourteenth-century glass, giving an impression of dark green, and Epstein's dramatic, twisting statue of Lazarus. Be sure not to miss the exquisite stained glass window by the famous eighteenth-century artist, Sir Joshua Reynolds. The artist portrayed himself as a shepherd. In the main body of the chapel, look to the left of the altar for the founder's silver-gilt pastoral staff kept behind glass. Scenes of architecture are contained in its metal. Look for the miniature gothic arches. Nearby is a painting by El Greco, of St. James. The chapel itself was largely rebuilt during the nineteenth century.

New College Garden is one of the delights of Oxford. From the front quad proceed into the garden quad, then through the superb early eighteenth-century wrought iron gates emblazoned with the college crest and motto "Manners Makyth Man." The extensive garden is L-shaped and stretches off to the right beyond the tree-covered mound more than three hundred years old. To your left the battlements and bastions of the original medieval city wall provide an historic background for the luxurious herbaceous border. The city wall was an important defense during the civil war of the 1640s, when the increasingly beleaguered Charles I had his base in Oxford. The cloisters you have just seen were used then to store cannon balls. From the corner of the garden near the wall to the left of the entrance gates, you have an unusual view of **Magdalen Tower.**

From New College gate turn left under the arch and walk along narrow Queen's Lane that twists between high stone walls. In a moment you pass on your right the new Provost's Lodge of **The Queen's College.** From the lane it presents a fortresslike appearance with spikes from the time before coeducation, when students had to leave college for their nightlife.

About twenty-five yards before the lane reaches a busy street, **the High,** turn left into the narrow entrance of **St. Edmund Hall.** Since this college is not one of Oxford's most visited, and the architecture is delightful rather than spectacular, this is a good place to linger and explore.

Just inside the quad look left for officially tolerated graffiti, in chalk, commemorating the college's athletic success. One recent chalk sign here boasted of the college's Women's First VIII (rowers), who had "bumped" other college crews. The "bumps" races have a staggered start; to defeat the crew in front, your bow must come level with their stern. (The boats are too expensive these days for a literal bump to be permitted.) The cult of the athlete, the "hearty," was strong in Oxford and Cambridge from Victorian times till World War II. In the 1960s and 1970s it languished; a dominant socialist ethos among undergraduates despised such upper-class luxury as a university education frittered away in sport. Now the hearties are back. You may look in vain for an idealistic bit of graffiti.

On the far side of the quad are the **Corinthian columns** of the chapel (from 1682), pleasantly human rather than grand in scale. (If you prefer the grander style, there will be Queen's College in a moment.) Walk round the quad to see the **open staircases.** Such staircases are the basic domestic unit in Oxford and Cambridge. ("I'm in x quad on y staircase.") Look at the eighteenth-century lead drainpipes, and the **hand pump** from the same century. It bears the three feathers badge of the Prince of Wales, and the date 1783. Next to it, in 1995, we could see chalk graffiti, no doubt lovingly renewed, from 1965, when the college VIII had been "Head of the River" (top rowers of the university). Athleticism is the chief pride of St. Edmund Hall.

Go through the arch of Staircase No. 1 to the churchyard of St. Peter-in-the-East. The former church is now the college library. Notice the fine yew trees. The tradition of growing yew trees in churchyards supposedly dates from the Middle Ages. Yew berries are poisonous to cattle and so must be kept away from open fields. But yew was needed, because from its wood were made the finest long-bows, remembered as the most effective weapon against the French.

Back at the entrance to St. Edmund Hall, turn left into Queen's Lane, then right into the High for a famous view of the classic façade of Queen's and the broad curve of the High with the tall spire of St. Mary's rising above the tower of All Souls.

Thirty yards from Queen's Lane, on the right, are steps leading to The Queen's College. Pause for a moment to view the **clock tower** outlined by the entrance archway against the background of the sky. Founded in 1340 by Robert de Eglesfield, chaplain to Queen Philippa, wife of Edward III, Queen's as you see it today was rebuilt in the late seventeenth and early eighteenth centuries. Nicholas Hawksmoor was the chief architect of the splendid **front quad** which is cloistered on three sides. Directly ahead as you stand at the gate beyond the unbelievably smooth lawn stands the palatial façade of the college hall on the left and chapel on the right. The grandeur of Queen's excludes intimacy. The cloisters, even in fine weather, are not places to linger. As with so much eighteenth-century architecture, the purpose was to overawe rather than to produce comfort.

If you enter Queen's, head for the middle arch on the far side of the quad, but approach it by the cloister along the left of the quad, rather than directly.

The architectural glory of Queen's is the magnificent **west façade of the library,** one of the finest in Oxford. Go through the front quad and turn left in the early eighteenth-century back quad. The east front of the library with its tall windows is most impressive. Go under the arches by the library entrance to see the west façade, and then the contrasting intimacy of the little walled lane beyond it.

Wander along the walled passage next to the Provost's garden and turn left into the old **Nun's Garden,** a quiet corner of Oxford attractively planted with rose bushes and flowering trees. **Drawda Hall** facing the garden is an example of domestic architecture prevalent at the end of the seventeenth century.

Turn left from Queen's down the High toward **Magdalen** (pronounced Maudlin), whose magnificent bell tower looms ahead. Enter the college through the gatehouse on the left.

Just inside the college grounds (which comprise one hundred acres and are the largest in Oxford) you will see an **open-air pulpit,** one of very few surviving in England.

Go through the entrance beneath it. In the next courtyard, go through the entrance in the far left corner—opposite to the chapel tower. In the cloisters, go right and up wooden stairs to the distinguished **dining hall.** Its marvelous linenfold paneling, fine Jacobean screen, oriel window, and portraits of distinguished old members of the college, including a fine painting of Cardinal Wolsey, make the hall perhaps the most beautiful in Oxford. Note the woodcarving and Henry VIII's coat of arms over the high table.

Now walk to the opposite end of the cloisters. When you emerge, go right to tall iron gates. Immediately beyond them is a stone bridge leading to extensive parkland walks.

From the stone bridge go straight ahead, with the cloisters on your left and the eighteenth-century New Buildings on your right. At the far end of the New Buildings is a deer park; notice how saplings are fenced to protect their bark from the deers' teeth.

Back through the college, on the High once more, go left to Magdalen Bridge. Go down to the left, just before the bridge, to find where punts are hired (by the hour). If you try for yourself, first watch for a moment the arm movements of someone already punting. In handling the long pole, there are only three serious tips. Don't press the pole very hard into the river bottom, or it might just get stuck. Keep the pole as close as possible to vertical; if it meets the river bottom at a sharp angle it may skid and cause you to lose balance. To help the steering, trail the pole behind the punt as a rudder. Punting for the first time is almost always a success. Downstream (to the right) from Magdalen Bridge, between meadows and under a canopy of trees, is perhaps the finest place in the world to learn.

⚓ Oxford II

Start this walk close to where the last walk ended: at the entrance to Magdalen College, a few yards from Magdalen Bridge. From the college entrance, cross the main road (the High), go right for ten yards and then left into **Rose Lane.** Look right for the magnificent fanlight over the building at the corner of Rose Lane and the High. Walk two hundred yards along Rose Lane, go through the iron gates and turn right at the cottage, twenty yards beyond the gates.

There now opens to your right a lovely skyline, which includes **Tom Tower,** the landmark which is part of the college (and cathedral) known as **Christ Church.** Your path will take you along the edge of Christ Church Meadow, following the back walls of several colleges. Twenty yards beyond the cottage, look for a plaque in the wall which records that from the meadow here was launched the hot-air balloon of James Sadler, on October 4th, 1784, who thereby became "the first English astronaut."

After about three hundred yards is the back of **Merton College,** behind ornate spikes. (The meadow here would be an excellent, private place for climbing into college after an illicit late night.) Past Merton, follow the path through a ninety-degree turn. Then after two hundred yards turn right, still following the back walls of the college gardens. Fifty yards past this final bend look right, through a gate, into the garden. Ahead of you is **Corpus Christi College,** to the left Christ Church. From Christ Church, where he was a mathematics don, Charles Dodgson used to set out on walks across the meadow to the Thames with his young friend Alice Liddell and her sisters. He was Lewis Carroll, she was Alice in Wonderland.

Continue straight ahead to the gates and the main road (St. Aldate's): turn right and after one hundred fifty yards you are at the main entrance to Christ Church. This is the most majestic of all the colleges, and also has the undergraduates of grandest background. It is known in Oxford speech simply as the "House." Before entering the great gate with its tremendous oak doors, pause for a few minutes across St. Aldate's in the street leading to Pembroke College so you can study Tom Tower above the gateway.

Cardinal Wolsey, founder of Christ Church, completed the tower's massive base to the height of the flanking Tudor turrets. Then in 1681 Wren added the octagonal and pinnacled cupola with its Gothic ogee windows behind which hangs the huge bell, "Great Tom," cast in 1680 and weighing over six tons. When the hands of the tower clock show 9:05 each evening, the great bell booms 101 times. 100 for each of the original students plus one added in 1667. Today Christ Church has the largest number of students of all the colleges.

As you enter the **gateway** look above you to see the forty-eight coats of arms of prominent benefactors, including Henry VIII and Wolsey, which decorate the roof.

When you step into **Tom Quad,** you will be spellbound by its simple splendor. Cross the broad expanse of lawn to the stone terrace past the central pool with its statue of Mercury. You will notice that the arches and pillars built in the walls on the four sides of the quad indicate that Wolsey planned a cloister to encircle the court. From this point you can appreciate the grandeur of Tom Tower and its court. You may happen to be here when the quad is empty and a serene stillness accentuates its enormous scale.

From Tom Tower, the entry to the cathedral is in the side of the quad ahead of you, near the junction with the quad's right side. The cathedral is Oxford's most beautiful church with one of the oldest spires in England, which you can see well from the gateway of Tom Quad. Several features of the cathedral will catch your attention— the twelfth-century Norman pillars, the lovely fifteenth-century choir vaulting, and the double arches of the nave. In addition to the seventeenth-century vice-chancellor's throne and a Jacobean pulpit, there are several interesting old tombs and monuments. The small fifteenth-century cloisters are worth seeing.

From the cathedral entrance, turn left for a few yards to the entrance of the hall, with its **Great Staircase.** Take your time going up the Staircase with its great lanterns so you can study the remarkable **fan tracery** in the roof, a superb example of stone craftsmanship. The **Great Hall** at the top of the wide stone staircase is Oxford's largest. The lofty hammerbeam oak roof is richly carved and gilded. Christ Church's interesting collection of portraits, the finest in any Oxford college hall, adorn the paneled walls. Reynolds, Gainsborough, Romney, and Lawrence are represented. In addition to Henry VIII, Elizabeth I, and Wolsey, noted subjects include John Locke, C. L. Dodgson ("Lewis Carroll"), a former canon of Christ Church, and William Penn, an old member.

As you stand with your back to Tom Tower, in the far left corner of Tom Quad is the **Deanery.** (The Dean of Christ Church is the head of the college. Alice Liddell was daughter of a dean.) Here lodged Charles I during the civil war of the 1640s; London was controlled by his enemies, the Parliament. Just left of the Deanery is an archway. Go through it into **Peckwater Quad,** an excellent example of the Palladian style. The magnificent **library** on your right, recently refaced, now has a delicate tawny coloring but unfortunately is closed to the public. It houses the finest collection of paintings owned by any Oxford college. Just beyond the library is an iron gate. Go through it: twenty yards dead ahead of the gate is the entrance to **Corpus Christi College** ("Corpus," to Oxonians). Go through the quad to the gardens at the rear. Here, under trees, look out over the walled garden below to **Christ Church Meadow.** This is a lovely, and little-known, spot.

Back at the entrance to Corpus turn left as you leave the college, and then right, into Oriel Square. The entrance to **Oriel College** is on the right of the square. The projecting oriel window, directly above the entrance, gave the college its name. One of its best-known members was Cecil Rhodes, founder of the Rhodes Scholarships at Oxford. Go through the entrance to see, at the far end of the quad, a statue of the doomed Charles I, made in his lifetime: *Regnante Carolo* ("in Charles's reign") say large letters. Remember the similarly prominent statue of Charles's father James I, by the Bodleian library (Oxford Walk I). The disastrous Stuart dynasty, to which they belonged, was dogged by plots and civil wars. These assertions in stone may reflect their insecurity.

From Oriel Square go left, and left again, and one hundred yards ahead at the end of a street barred to traffic, you will see the **Bear Inn.** One of Oxford's most attractive pubs, it dates from the thirteenth century. In the Bear's oak-beamed bar, with an extraordinary collection of three thousand club ties in cases around the walls, you can enjoy a snack or a drink.

From the Bear Inn, walk along Alfred Street to the High. Twenty yards to the left, and across the High, is the entry to the **covered market.** This intimate place is well worth remembering for the friendly and extremely popular greasy spoon café, where dons, undergraduates, and visiting scholars with no base in Oxford go for large breakfasts. You will need to hunt for it among the numerous stalls and passageways of the market. This homely, animated spot makes a good place to end the walk, before you go on to more of Oxford's grand sights.

St. David's and Solva ✠

The small cathedral town of **St. David's** and the village of **Solva** are together at the world's end, at the southwesterly tip of Wales. Each is in a sunny, sheltered place, yet within a short walk are beaches and cliffs open to the power of the Atlantic. At St. David's you can explore the elaborate and friendly ruins of a **medieval palace,** a bishop's home from the 1300s. Bishops in those days were powerful and rich; the palace in reality is a castle. Solva, three miles away, has the air of a pretty **fishing village,** at the head of a winding creek. After visiting the peaceful lanes and corners of the village, you can follow a path along the creek to a headland overlooking a great sweep of islands and beaches.

The railway from London (Paddington station) will bring you to Haverfordwest—sixteen miles from St. David's. Buses go from Haverfordwest to St. David's, via Solva. But buses in west Wales are not frequent. St. David's was a place of remote pilgrimage in the Middle Ages, and is becoming so again! A car is advised, unless you plan to stay in the area.

St. David's

Begin at St. David's in the car park by the old **Bishop's Palace.** Beside you here is the little river **Alun** (pronounced "Alin"), whose waters no doubt caused the site to be chosen for settlement. St. David himself, a legendary founder of Welsh Christianity and now the patron saint of Wales, is believed to have established a community of monks in the area in the A.D. 500s. Bishop Henry de Gower was living here in style and security by the early 1300s, as you will see.

Twenty yards from the car park you reach the outer "**precinct**" **wall** of the palace. This is probably from the 1300s. Cross the stone bridge and walk up a gentle hill for a few yards, with the precinct wall on your left. Look back at the remains of a **fortified tower** at the edge of the river—a vulnerable spot. Notice the slits in the stonework, for archers. Sixty yards up the hill, turn left into the lane signposted, in Welsh, Eglwys Cadeiriol—"Cathedral Church." ("Eglwys" is from the Latin word for church: *ecclesia*.) Once in the lane, look left to appreciate the strength of the wall: at this point its walkway and battlements are almost intact.

Who was the enemy against whom these mighty fortifications were needed? Bishop de Gower had the wealth for some pretty architecture—you will soon see the famous **arcaded parapets** decorating his castle. But it's very unlikely that he had the wealth to gird his large site with this mighty precinct wall just for decoration. The guide books are rather vague as to who the enemy was. There are occasional references to Viking pirates, but by the 1300s there were no more wicked Vikings. In reality the enemy was the Welsh. The sunny and rich coastal lowlands of Pembrokeshire had been captured from the Welsh by Normans. (Notice the "*de*" in Bishop de Gower's name, a trace of Norman French.) Welsh-speakers in the hills of north Pembrokeshire and beyond probably

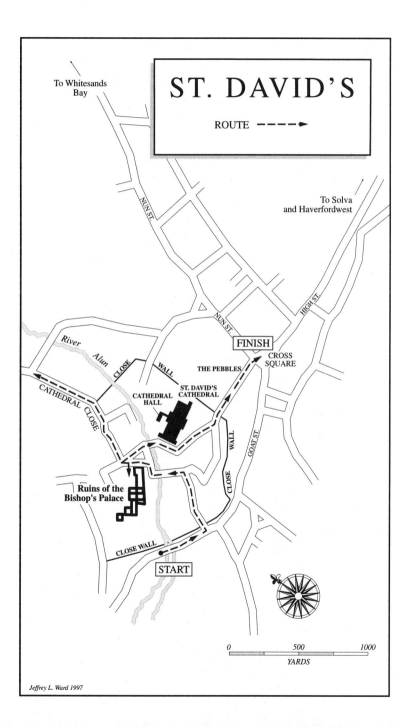

ST. DAVID'S

ROUTE ----▶

To Whitesands
Bay

To Solva
and Haverfordwest

NUN ST.

NUN ST.

HIGH ST.

River
Alun

CLOSE

WALL

FINISH

CROSS
SQUARE

CATHEDRAL CLOSE

THE PEBBLES

ST. DAVID'S
CATHEDRAL

CATHEDRAL
HALL

CLOSE WALL

GOAT ST.

Ruins of the
Bishop's Palace

CLOSE WALL

START

0   500   1000
YARDS

Jeffrey L. Ward 1997

saw these wealthy settlements on their coasts as alien, well worth raiding.

Walk one hundred yards farther along the lane, until you reach a junction: across the road is the entry to the cathedral grounds. But turn left here and go downhill thirty yards toward the large road sign saying "Ford." **Ford** over the **river Alun,** that is. You now have a fine view of the ruined Bishop's Palace, with the arcaded parapets above, the stone skeleton of a "wheel window" to the left, and round chimneys to the right. For monasteries like this, the death-blow was given by Henry VIII in the 1530s, when he broke from Rome and seized church property. But the monastery here seems to have died gently, its buildings not utterly plundered by new land-lords wishing to re-use the stone. Henry VIII's family, the Tudors, came from Wales. It is guessed that royal sentiment about this Welsh connection protected St. David's from rough treatment.

Cross the footbridge over the river. Some smooth boulders on your left make good temporary seats while you take in the view of the palace. Now head for the entrance gate to the palace, a few yards away on your right. (On the way is the exceptionally discreet entrance to a public toilet.) Inside the gateway there is an admission charge to pay. The shop here sells a cheap and extremely well produced guide book with color photos, which makes a good souvenir. (Its title is *St. David's Bishop's Palace.*)

Inside the gateway you are on the lawn of the main palace court-yard. On the far side is the tall ruin of the **Great Hall,** with **colon-naded arcade** along the top. First, go just to the left of the guardhouse to explore a dark, vaulted room on the ground floor—and undercroft. Look for a narrow stone staircase to take you up one floor, from where you can make your way from room to room. First is the bishop's **private chapel,** then his **solar**—a place for relax-ing with favored guests after a feast in the Great Hall. As you explore the roofless chambers of the palace, look out for postholes in the walls. These show where timbers were supported, and so give you an idea of where ceilings and floors once were. Also look for the **ornamental sculpted heads** set high in the walls.

The best way to reach the Great Hall is the route by which the bishop and his guests used to enter. Go back to the lawn of the main courtyard and look for the elaborate arch of purple stone which leads into the Hall. The arch is approached by stone steps. We can imagine the clerics and courtiers in their finery sweeping in. Above the stone arch are the ruins of a coat of arms (center) and (left and right) two niches for statues.

Once inside the Great Hall, look up for a moment once more at the wheel window. Then walk to the opposite end of the Hall where, on the left, a winding stair will take you to the level of the parapet, above the arches. Up here, with the wind and the jackdaws (small, hooded crows), there is a lovely view over the whole medieval site. Look over to the near edge of the modern town, just right of the cathedral, to see the stone **Tower Gate,** which looks like a small castle in its own right. Once there were four such gates, all massively fortified, in the outer precinct wall. (You will be passing though the Tower Gate in a few minutes.)

Back on the ground, from inside the Great Hall make your way to see where the bishop's feasts were prepared. The kitchen is near the wheel window. If you stand below the wheel window, outside the Great Hall, check to see if there are still molehills in the lawn.

When you leave the palace, from the gateway go along the lane which starts opposite the gateway and a few yards to the left. Here, in big houses of Georgian and Victorian style, live some of today's top clerics. Elegant walled gardens act as sheltered sun-traps. But in the treetops just behind, in most weathers, is the howl of the Atlantic wind. Walk three hundred yards along this lane to a stone bridge over the Alun. Here is a sign directing resolute walkers the couple of miles to dramatic **Whitesands Bay,** with its seascape of rocky islands.

Retrace your steps down the lane. Just before you reach the entrance to the Bishop's Palace, turn left along the cobbled pathway which leads toward the cathedral. The path goes over a bridge: stop for a moment to admire the river as it runs between stone walls. Then on to the **cathedral.** If you go inside, look for the grave of Bishop Henry de Gower, the shaper of the palace. He lies near the east (altar) end of the nave, behind iron railings. The medieval stone effigy above the grave shows the bishop in his mitre. The great stone arches supporting the nave are in the rounded, Norman style—ultimately borrowed from the Romans. They were built in the late 1100s. Contrast them with the more common, later style of arch—the pointed, Gothic, sort which you can also see here. Above the great arches in the nave are simple, attractive windows in the Norman manner. Look up to the (more recent) fine woodwork in the ceiling of the nave.

From the cathedral, walk uphill to the mighty Tower Gate, noting on the way how the treetops to your right slope away from the prevailing westerly winds. Under the arch of Tower Gate stop to look for the slot which once held the portcullis, the iron grille against intruders. Ancient iron studs rust here in forgotten doorways.

From Tower Gate continue uphill, past shops selling tea and souvenirs, and into the town's main street. Ahead of you is a high stone cross. To the left of it is the very pleasant **Old Cross hotel**—and pub.

Solva

Start your walk at the head of the creek, by the **Harbour House Pub.** On both sides are hills glittering with yellow gorse. Before exploring the creek and going up to the headland beyond, have a look at the village of Solva (strictly "lower Solva"—there is another, larger, section of Solva uphill on the road to St. David's).

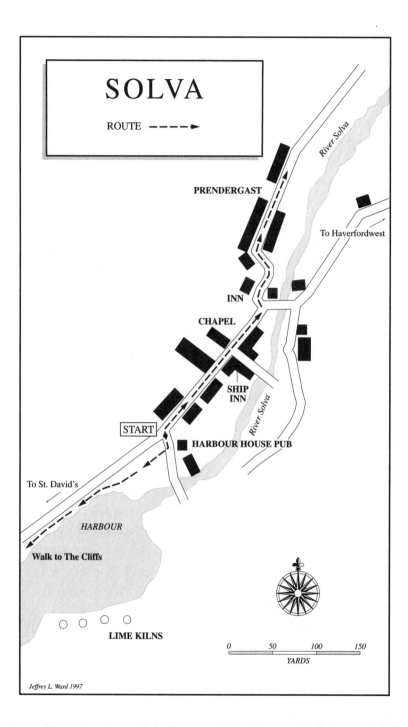

SOLVA

ROUTE ----→

PRENDERGAST

River Solva

To Haverfordwest

INN

CHAPEL

SHIP
INN

START

HARBOUR HOUSE PUB

River Solva

To St. David's

HARBOUR

Walk to The Cliffs

LIME KILNS

| 0 | 50 | 100 | 150 |
YARDS

Jeffrey L. Ward 1997

From the Harbour House turn into the village street, with its houses painted in Georgian pastel colors. Look in particular for pink. On Welsh cottages the color pink came into fashion around 1800. In England fashion swiftly moved on; here the style remained and is now worn proudly as a badge of rural Welshness. Fifty yards along the village street, on the right, is the delightful **Ship Inn.** Here, or at the Harbour House, is the place to relax after your walk. Just past the Ship, turn right for a moment to explore a path which leads between cottages to the little river Solva. Beyond a footbridge is a children's playground.

Back in the main street, opposite you is an impressive stone building, once a warehouse and now catering to visitors. Cross to it, then go twenty yards farther along the street, to reach a (former) **Non-Conformist chapel.** Wales, until the 1980s, had many thousands of functioning chapels, mostly dating from the nineteenth century. It has been seriously argued that in the 1800s Non-Conformism, and especially Methodism, kept Britain from revolution—by directing high hopes to the next world rather than to this one. The religion of the chapels in Wales caused the near-extinction of the riotous local folk culture, which had involved much dancing, drinking, and the production of unplanned babies. Such things were Sin. Denunciations of individual sinners from the chapel pulpit are still remembered. In English minds, the image of Wales still includes the tall, slate-roofed chapel in the rain, where a gaunt elderly preacher excitedly condemns the blooming but disgraced figure of some maiden-no-more. Today, for lack of believers, the chapels are going—demolished, converted into houses or, like this one, into shops for visitors. And in the schools of Wales, while religion may be half-hearted, there are enthusiastic attempts to revive the *twmpath,* the evening of musical revelry which the chapels stamped out.

Past the chapel, the main road bears right, over a bridge, uphill and out of the village. Before the bridge, take the fork to the left, passing in front of The Cambrian pub (*"Cambria"* is a Latin version of the Welsh word for Wales, *Cymru*). The village street, or rather "lane," here passes between delightful cottages, some with gardens built into the steep hillside, others with lawns leading down to the river. Walk along a few hundred yards to the end of the cottages. The position of this little settlement was well chosen. The gardens point south, and all are sheltered from the prevailing westerly winds. Even the wind from the sea is blocked by the creek of Solva, which curves conveniently.

Walk back now the length of the village to the point where you started, by the Harbour House Pub. (The food at the pub is highly recommended.) After you turn from the main road into the carpark beside the pub, look to the right. Here, a few feet from the junction with the main road, are traces of a mighty, and highly successful, enterprise from Solva's past. This little village was once a place of industry. Trading ships came up the creek, lime kilns sent up clouds of dust, and here at the creek side were prepared the parts of a great lighthouse—some of them are now before you.

Out in the Atlantic, some twenty-three miles from Solva, is a reef called **the Smalls.** In the 1700s ships approaching the growing port of Liverpool were often wrecked on it. A competition was launched to design a lighthouse for the rocks. The winner was a young maker of musical instruments from Liverpool, Henry Whiteside. His design was for a hut on iron stilts. For greater flexibility he replaced some of the metal with wood, and finished his lighthouse in 1775. Some of the discarded metal sections are now at your feet. Also here is a block of granite from Cornwall, glittering with particles in the stone. This was brought to make a replacement lighthouse, taller, stronger, and brighter, in the mid-nineteenth century. The stone for the new structure was prepared by the creek here.

Tales were told of the sufferings borne by the early lighthouse-keepers in Whiteside's hut-on-stilts. Once the water ran low, and messages in bottles were thrown into the sea appealing for help—successfully! Another time a lighthouse keeper died, and his colleague was left for days on his own with the body. But there was an immense saving of lives through the prevention of shipwreck. Ships reaching Liverpool paid a toll toward the lighthouse, which had been privately financed. The venture was enormously profitable. Whiteside himself, no doubt by this time a local hero, settled down in the village and married the daughter of the man who ran the Ship Inn.

Begin your walk to the sea by going through the carpark toward the creek, which will be on your left. About two hundred yards from the pub, look across the creek to the row of abandoned lime kilns on the far side—low, rounded structures of stone. Three hundred yards farther, beside your path and in a place where yachts are parked, is a hut of yellow brick, with an ancient metal plate advertising Spiller's dog food. This building was used for storage in the days when steamboats sailed at high tide from here to Bristol. The last building you reach on this quay was once a lifeboat shed; look for the commemorative plaque on the wall.

A few feet beyond the old lifeboat shed take the pathway that climbs the hillside. A wooden sign directs you: "**Coast path.**" After a few yards the path forks. Go for a moment to the left. Twenty yards along there is a **seat with a view** over the mouth of the creek. It was views like this which made us include Solva in your itinerary. You may notice that great rocks at the river mouth shelter the creek from the full force of the sea.

Now go back to the fork in the path and take the other route—uphill and heading for the house with a red spire. Walk in front of the house—on the side facing the creek. Don't be put off by the private-looking gate you pass. You may notice, immediately before the gate, a wooden peg in the ground on your left bearing the logo of a yellow acorn, to reassure walkers, discreetly but firmly, that this is indeed the public coastal path. (You may guess that there has been psychological warfare here, between private owners and the authorities who administer the path.) Pass in front of the house and go almost straight ahead to the narrow entry, amid hawthorn bushes, to a rough and narrow track. The hedges on either side of the track gradually are replaced by grassy banks. The track reaches a wooden gateway into a field. Go through the gate, walk along the left side of the field until, just before the corner of the field, another gate leads you away to the left. Once through this gate you are on the headland. From the rocky outcrop ahead of you there is a dramatic view over the beaches and rocks of **St. Brides Bay,** and a gentler view back along the creek to Solva itself.

Useful phone numbers:
Tourist Information, Haverfordwest (for bus times to St. David's and Solva): 01437 763110
Old Cross Hotel, St. David's: 01437 720387

✤ SALISBURY

A prosperous country town of extraordinary beauty, **Salisbury** has a sophisticated welcome for visitors but has not surrendered to mass tourism. Its historical charms are many but subtle. There is no single obvious tourist attraction, other than the **cathedral.** And even the cathedral, from the inside, is elegantly simple and uncluttered, giving an effect of airy grace rather than the colorful, crowded intensity of many "top" cathedrals. But set in the simplicity of the cathedral are artworks of rare beauty. The cathedral itself is surrounded by spacious lawns and historic dwelling houses—in the **Cathedral Close.** Outside the close, the town is still in recognizably medieval form, with narrow streets and ancient buildings. And on the edge of the town, only a couple of minutes' walk from the cathedral, the clear waters of the rivers **Avon** and **Nadder** run through meadows where you will walk to a quiet pub which overlooks a millpool. As a setting for a country pub, we know of nowhere in Britain more beautiful.

You can easily reach Salisbury from London by road or rail. It is quickest to take the fast train from Waterloo, and you will be in Salisbury in about an hour and three-quarters.

If you are driving to Salisbury, the cathedral's lofty spire, a famous landmark in this part of the country, will be visible for miles around.

On arrival in the town, go directly to the **cathedral close.** Pause for a few moments by the green to absorb the mood of this lovely scene—the lines of the great gray Gothic cathedral, its lofty **spire** that rises over four hundred feet (the highest church spire in England), the broad expanse of lawn encircled by a fourteenth-century stone wall, and the charming Georgian brick houses that surround the spacious close.

The most perfectly proportioned example of early English Gothic style, Salisbury Cathedral is an architectural classic. The only English cathedral of uniform design, it was begun in 1220 and completed thirty-eight years later. The tower and spire are fourteenth century.

After strolling about the close to view the cathedral from different angles, enter the building (admission fee). At once you will be struck by the somber effect of the interior—perhaps due to the dark Purbeck marble. Although the superb proportions and harmonious design of the cathedral's interior will impress you, perhaps you will not sense the same excitement as when you studied its exceptional exterior.

Turn to your left on entering the cathedral to view the great **west window.** It contains some of the finest and oldest glass in the cathedral, much of it thirteenth century. Cross the **nave** to the north door. Close to the door is the clanking mechanism of a clock dating from 1386, or a little earlier, and still with many of its original parts. Near the clock hang flags—all faded, some dwindled to skeletons—of

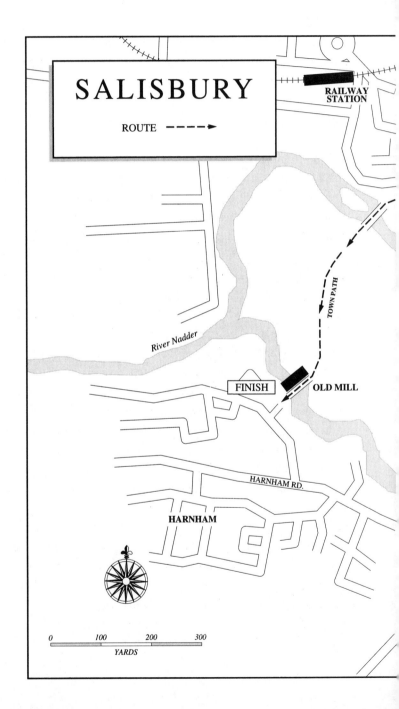

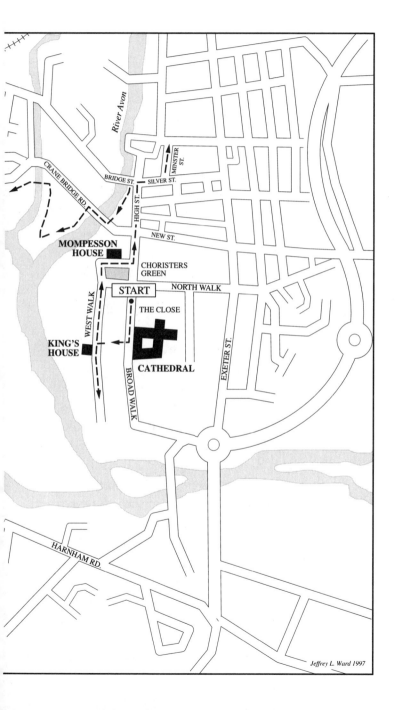

River Avon

CRANE BRIDGE RD.

BRIDGE ST.   SILVER ST.

MINSTER ST.

HIGH ST.

NEW ST.

MOMPESSON HOUSE

CHORISTERS GREEN

WEST WALK

NORTH WALK

START

THE CLOSE

KING'S HOUSE

CATHEDRAL

EXETER ST.

BROAD WALK

HARNHAM RD.

Jeffrey L. Ward 1997

bygone regiments of the British empire. On the other side of the north door, set in the wall is a moving **portrait** in stone of a nineteen-year-old officer killed in 1916 at the battle of the Somme. A few yards away is the medieval effigy of a knight, his feet resting on a lion. This was Sir John de Montacute, who fought the French at the battle of Crécy and died in 1390. The legend on his **tomb** tells that he was King of the Isle of Man. As you wander down the nave, you will admire the graceful **arcades.** In the center of the cathedral directly below the spire you will find in the stone flooring a **brass tablet** indicating that the spire leans twenty-nine and a half inches to the southwest. As you stand at the plaque, facing the altar and the **east window,** look up at the pillar on your right. You will see that it bends to the right as it climbs. The two stone bridges which you see here under the spire, running east-west, were built in the fifteenth century to stop the movement of the structure. So were the **arches** which you see behind the original arcades.

Go right and head for the east window. After passing the high altar look for the superb stone effigies of a pair of Tudor aristocrats. The wife (died 1563) was Lady Katherine Grey; the husband (died 1621) was Thomas Seymour, Earl of Hertford. Both had royal connections, and so were lucky to survive amid the plots of Tudor England. Thomas was a relative of Jane Seymour, Henry VIII's third wife. A relative also named Thomas Seymour had been beheaded for high treason. Katherine, even more perilously, was a descendant of Henry VII. After Queen Elizabeth she was next in line of succession. Her elder sister, the courageous and tragic young scholar Jane Grey, was executed in 1554 at the age of sixteen, after being put forward as queen, for nine days, by rebels against Catholic Mary Tudor. As a married couple, Katherine and Thomas must have seemed a dangerous combination, if only as unwilling instruments in the plots of others. The monument here, with its Latin inscription, gives an impression of serene love between the two. In fact they spent much time in prison, the young Queen Elizabeth having been alarmed by their secret wedding. Together in the Tower of London they managed to communicate—in fact to conceive a child. The Queen's anger must have been intensified by this. Katherine was kept in prison until she died. Her letters to the Queen, begging to be allowed to see her husband, were in vain.

Katherine is shown here as fashionably dressed and intensely beautiful. She wears a Tudor ruff at the neck. Her profile, especially the delicate nose, is superb. The effigy was made long after her death and is very likely idealized, but it is still one of the best clues as to the appearance of her charismatic sister, the Protestants' lost Queen Jane.

Retrace your steps until you are level with the pulpit, under the steeple. Then turn left into the south transept: A door in the corner to your right leads to the cloisters and to the **Chapter House.** Go in. In keeping with the cathedral proper, the works of art on show in the Chapter House are few and magnificent. Here you will see the most perfect of the four originals of **Magna Carta** (of 1215). (The one with the actual signatures no longer exists.) Written on vellum—animal skin—in Latin, the lettering still stands out with calligraphic precision. Look at the translation (in the Chapter House's entry passage) to get some idea of the chaotic corruption and social oppression under King John, which the barons hoped their document would rectify: "No widow shall be compelled to marry so long as she prefers to live without a husband . . ."—"We will at once release the son of Llywelyn and all Welsh hostages. . . ." Sometimes on exhibit is the autographed survey of the cathedral by Sir Christopher Wren whose recommendations saved the spire. Other treasures are a remarkable **tenth-century psalter,** in old English, books from **William Caxton's** fifteenth-century press, a description and map of **Virginia** by Captain John Smith (printed in 1612), and **William Harvey's book** on the circulation of the blood (1628). To be sure of seeing a particular exhibit, write beforehand to the cathedral's librarian. The Chapter House itself is octagonal. The vaulted roof springs from the central pillars in keeping with its late thirteenth-century style. Be sure to study the remarkable **thirteenth-century sculptures,** illustrating scenes from the Books of Genesis and Exodus, in the canopied arcading around the wall. These sculptured groups are among the most unusual of their kind to be seen in any Gothic cathedral. Enter the thirteenth-century **cloisters,** the largest and perhaps the most beautiful in England. Two tall magnificent cedars of Lebanon in the center of the lawn contribute to the monastic atmosphere. At the far corner, glance upward through the traceried arches for a fine view of the tower and spire. From the cloisters you will leave the cathedral, close to the point by which you entered. From the exit, with your back to the great west window, walk ahead across the wide lawn to **West Walk.** Turn left, to stroll by the walled front gardens of lovely Georgian mansions. Behind their back gardens, as a natural moat, runs the **River Avon**—you will reach it later. From the front here, notice the view of the cathedral spire rising from behind trees. Retracing your steps on West Walk, opposite the cathedral, look for the King's House, now the Salisbury and South Wiltshire **Museum,** with a welcome tea shop. Immediately beyond the Museum is the eighteenth-century **Audley House,** with superb fanlights and mellowed red brick. Past Audley House look for the **North Canonry,** with high ancient doors and leaded windows in stone frames. Parts of this building appear to be of Tudor date. In a house just beyond, the elder statesman Edward Heath (Prime Minister 1970–74) lived from the 1980s. A Conservative, and a soldier in World War II, he was notably keener than Mrs. Thatcher on the rights of the common people and on harmony between European states.

Continue along West Walk, passing attractive dark red brick houses with white windows set back behind flower-filled gardens to the green or "choristers square." Here is the most elegant house of all, **Mompesson House.** Built in 1701, the interior of this exquisitely decorated and furnished home (open in the summer 12:00–5:30; closed Thursdays and Fridays) is quite exceptional. The splendid paneling, lovely plaster work, and beautiful furniture make this home (which is still lived in) one of the most tasteful examples of an eighteenth-century house. From the front, look up at the lead drainpipes: at the top is molded the date at which the house was built.

As you walk from the door of Mompesson House, turn left and leave the cathedral close by a gateway building also on the left. Just before the gateway, on the right, is a superb almshouse of stone and brick, bearing the date 1682. Once through the gateway, in **High Street** walk straight ahead for about two hundred yards until you reach **Silver Street.** Cross Silver Street then look to the right for **St. Thomas's Church,** founded in 1238, largely of fifteenth-century construction. Its nave has an extremely fine **Tudor roof.** The great **fresco** above the chancel arch is an unusual fifteenth-century painting of the Last Judgment.

Returning to Silver Street, go left along the street, then ten yards around the first corner on the left into **Minster Street.** Across the road you will see the little market, a stone canopy on columns, called **Poultry Cross,** some six hundred years old. Right beside you is the **Haunch of Venison Inn,** known for beautiful cooking. It has two delightful little bars, one of them immediately inside the main door, the other, up a few stairs, is a "snug"—very small and with an air of privacy. The restaurant, on an upper floor, has exposed roof-beams and is said to be of medieval date.

Retrace your steps along Silver Street, then continue on **Bridge Street** for about one hundred yards. On reaching the bridge itself, turn left onto the path along the near side of the River Avon. In another one hundred yards or so you reach a fine stone bridge. Cross it and continue along the path which now runs on the far side of the river. Shortly you will be in open meadows. Across the river are the gardens of the fine houses you saw a while ago in Cathedral Close. Your path bends back on itself. Where it passes a children's playground, turn left over a wooden bridge. After two hundred yards or so, turn left to cross another bridge which will lead you to water meadows, intersected by irrigation channels. The flow of water in the channels is controlled by wooden hatches; look out for one beside your path. Ahead of you, in the distance, you may see a white quarry in the hillside. The famous clear streams of Wiltshire, famous for their trout, are known as "chalk streams." The Avon is one; shortly you will reach another, the Nadder.

As you cross the water meadows toward **Harnham Mill,** you will be among ducks, swans, and, in sunshine, butterflies. The mill is medieval, with sagging roof and worn stone windows in the pointed, gothic style familiar from churches. The River Nadder passes right underneath the mill, where it used to power three waterwheels. The river then rushes out below your feet into the millpool.

Take a seat overlooking the millrace. Away to your right is the immaculate thatched roof of a half-timbered cottage. And next to the old mill is a handsome red brick building of the eighteenth century which is now a hotel and pub—"The Old Mill." Its restaurant section is in the medieval mill itself. A passage between the two buildings leads to a peaceful and secluded beer garden on the bank of the Nadder. Here, in the private garden, or at the front overlooking the millpool, choose your place to relax, in the most luxurious peace England can offer.

STOW-ON-THE-WOLD ❧

Few villages are famous. **Stow** is one of the few, known for its lovely, yellow, stone houses, the "Cotswold stone," for the medieval feel of its streets, and for the surrounding countryside. We shall walk through both village and country.

Stow lies on a **Roman road,** the **Fosse Way,** which linked the fort of Cirencester to the Midlands. This was frontier territory for the Romans; the last good countryside before the barely penetrable Welsh hills. The *-cester* endings of place names, Gloucester, Cirencester, Worcester, show where Roman forts (*castra* in Latin) once stood. Stow grew where later Anglo-Saxon roads crossed the Fosse Way. It has been a rich place three times. First in the late Middle Ages, when wool merchants from continental Europe converged for the famous Cotswold fleeces. A road in the village is still called Sheep Street. The street is said to have contained the overflow of animals from the great market in the village square. Then, in the eighteenth century, the profits from the turnpike roads which met at Stow led to the creation of several fine buildings which you

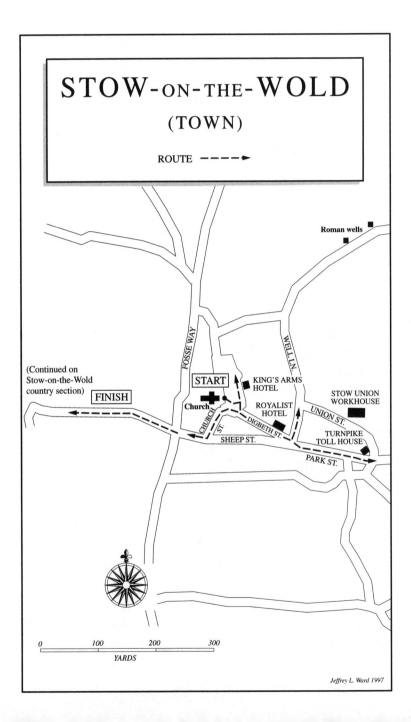

STOW-ON-THE-WOLD

(TOWN)

ROUTE - - - - ▶

Roman wells

FOSSE WAY

WELL LN.

(Continued on
Stow-on-the-Wold
country section)

START

KING'S ARMS
HOTEL

STOW UNION
WORKHOUSE

FINISH

Church

ROYALIST
HOTEL

UNION ST.

CHURCH ST.

DIGBETH ST.

TURNPIKE
TOLL HOUSE

SHEEP ST.

PARK ST.

0   100   200   300

YARDS

Jeffrey L. Ward 1997

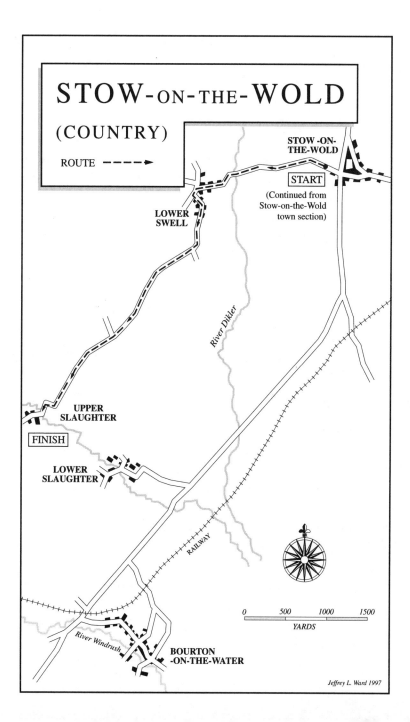

STOW-ON-THE-WOLD
(COUNTRY)

ROUTE ----▶

STOW -ON-
THE-WOLD

START

(Continued from
Stow-on-the-Wold
town section)

LOWER
SWELL

River Dikler

UPPER
SLAUGHTER

FINISH

LOWER
SLAUGHTER

RAILWAY

0   500   1000   1500

YARDS

River Windrush

BOURTON
-ON-THE-WATER

Jeffrey L. Ward 1997

will see. And today Stow has come to life again, as a favorite of prosperous visitors. Antique shops around the square gleam with the results of metal polish and beeswax. (The prices of antiques here are high enough to be mentioned in hushed tones.)

Start in the village square. Look for **St. Edward's House** (currently "**St. Edward's Café**") on the square's west side. This elegant town house has tall pilasters—inset columns—rising to a flourish of Corinthian art. The building is from the eighteenth century, when road tolls brought money to spare. Now, by the Grecian splendor, pigeons doze.

From where you stand, facing St. Edward's House, turn left and, on the same sidewalk, walk until the first turning on the right (**Church Street**). Go into Church Street and, after a few yards, go through the arched gateway on the right—and you are soon standing in the churchyard. The impressive tower is from the 1400s, much of the rest of the church is from the previous century. Wool from Cotswold sheep brought the wealth to make this building.

The church was the scene of an important episode in the English civil wars of the mid-1600s. King Charles I had abolished parliament, hoping thus to raise taxes without obstruction from the gentry. The gentry, and the poor, resisted and Charles declared war on them. By the mid-1640s Charles's power had shrunk to a small area of western England, around here. Stow, where the roads converged, became the eye of the storm. The king's last big garrisons were in Oxford, his own base southeast of Stow, and Worcester to the northwest. In March of 1646 a small army from Worcester, commanded by Sir Jacob Astley, was marching to Oxford to help the king. On March 21, Astley's men were brought to battle by parliamentarians on a hill just north of Stow. The battle spread into the village itself. The royalists surrendered. Over one thousand of them, it is said, were imprisoned for a night in this church, the best-fortified building in Stow. King Charles, deprived of his army of

Worcester, himself surrendered. After trying in vain to reopen civil war with the help of foreign mercenaries, he was beheaded in 1649.

Charles is commemorated in Stow as in few other places. While still at the head of glittering forces he himself visited the village several times. From the churchyard, retrace your route along Church Street into the square. On the far side from St. Edward's House is the **King's Arms Hotel.** Walk over to it, noticing on your way the medieval stone shaft of the cross in the marketplace. The King's Arms is named after Charles, who is recorded as staying here in May of 1645.

High on the handsome stone frontage of the King's Arms are the words "Posting House." This has nothing to do with modern mail. It refers to the pre-Victorian system of carrying mail by the use of horses in relays. In stables behind the hotel here fresh horses waited. Have a look through the gateway at the right of the hotel entrance, to see what is left of the stable yard.

From where you stand on the sidewalk facing the King's Arms turn right and, on the same sidewalk, leave the square and enter **Digbeth Street.** Walk on the left of this street until you reach the Royalist Hotel (and pub). This ancient building is reported to have a timber frame from the A.D. 900s. From outside, notice the small window in each side wall of the porch. These windows are remembered as hatches from which food was handed out to the poor and lepers. Customers of the pub are recommended to look carefully at the stonework of an old fireplace in what is now the restaurant. Enter the building through the porch, then take the first entrance to the left. This is the restaurant. Immediately inside, on the left, is the fireplace—look at its top left corner. Recently, layers of old decoration were removed to reveal small circles and other marks cut into the stone. These are interpreted as witches' marks—meant to prevent evil flying hags from gaining entrance through the chimney, as they evidently were prone to do! The Royalist Hotel is kept with pride and an enthusiasm for its history. It would make a fine setting in which to dine, or to stay.

Twenty yards farther down Digbeth Street is the turning, on the left, into **Well Lane.** You may like to walk a few hundred yards along Well Lane to see the lovely line of ten country cottages, Shepherd's Row, on the right. Alternatively, passing by the junction with Well Lane, continue downhill. Here Digbeth Street becomes **Park Street.** Walk until you reach the junction with Union Street, on the left. On the corner here is a turnpike toll house, from the 1700s. Note the arrangement of the wall and windows to allow vigilance in all directions.

The name "Union Street" would have had a chill ring to it in the 1800s. The Union, in full "Poor Law Union," meant the workhouse, where the destitute were supported, just, with a deliberately miserable regime of labor. Here, on the edge of the village, was the route to the workhouse, the road to ruin. Dickens made such places famous with *Oliver Twist.* Many adults remembered an orphaned childhood in the Union. For the elderly, here was the place for an impoverished death.

Retrace your route up Park and Digbeth Streets. Walk along the square again, on the sidewalk which passes the King's Arms. About one hundred yards beyond that pub is the White Hart pub. Turn for a moment to the right, under the arch by the pub. Here a winding cobbled lane leads to a beer garden. Notice the special strips in the cobbles, designed to protect against wear by the iron wheels of carts.

Cross the Square, passing St. Edward's Café once again, then turn right once more into Church St. This time continue onto **Sheep Street.** Turn right, passing the post office and the Unicorn Hotel until you reach traffic lights. Directly across the main road you will see a road marked Lower Swell and Naunton. There is a twenty-minute walk on this road—usually not heavily traveled—

first beside grassy banks and stone walls and then bordered by tall trees. The road descends from Stow on the hilltop to the valley of the **River Dikler,** a small stream which you cross just before reaching Lower Swell. If you turn right in the village, you will come to the **parish church,** which is partly Norman and built on the site of a Roman crematorium.

From the triangular green, in the center of the village, follow the road marked Upper Slaughter up a slight rise. Stow's church tower stands out prominently in the distance. At the fork you keep right on the narrow paved road. A great expanse of undulating country opens up on your left. Fields and woods dip down to the valley of the Dikler and rise to the far ridges. Here and there you will spot great manor houses and adjacent farm buildings. Along the top a strong breeze blows across the hills. You will feel invigorated both by the air and the lovely views both near and far over the beautiful Cotswold countryside. In a nearby field a spreading hawthorn stands in solitary splendor above a hedgerow. Continue along the crest and soon the road will begin to descend to Upper Slaughter. As you walk along this stretch there is a striking view of the valley in which the village lies on the banks of a little stream.

Upper Slaughter has been settled since the days of the early Britons before the Roman occupation.

After crossing the stream, keep to your left and you will pass a high wall. Behind this stands the **Lords of the Manor,** one of the finest manor houses in the Cotswolds, part Elizabethan and part fifteenth century. It has been converted into a hotel and restaurant. Bear right in the center of the village by the square and follow a little passage a bit farther on to the **parish church.** Originally built about 1160, the church is Norman and Early English in style. The fourteenth-century tower has one famous bell, called the "**Eleanor Bell,**" cast during the reign of King Edward I and his queen, Eleanor. Three of the chancel windows are of the fourteenth century. The churchyard, planted with clipped yews, overlooks the cottages and farm buildings along the winding streamside. In summer the gardens are ablaze with roses.

Useful phone numbers:
Tourist Information office, Stow: 01451 831082
Royalist Hotel: 01451 830670

TENBY ⚜

Tenby, in South West Wales, is one of the most beautiful towns of northern Europe, and is likely to remain that way. What keeps it little known is its distance from big cities. The oldest streets lie inside a **medieval town wall.** Ancient alleyways and lanes twist between cottages. Grander terraces of elegant houses from the nineteenth century look out over the sea. To the east they face a small harbor. To the south is a view of Caldey, a quiet island with a monastery. After walking in the town you may stroll along wide, sheltered beaches of sand, or in summer, take a boat across to the island for walks in near-solitude.

The best land on the southern coasts of Wales was seized by Normans and English in the Middle Ages. The Welsh were left with the badlands, the mountains, and rough ground where, until today, their language survives. Tenby, with its fine harbor, good farmland, and sheltered position, was guarded by a Norman castle on its headland. The Welsh swept in repeatedly in the 1100s and 1200s, to

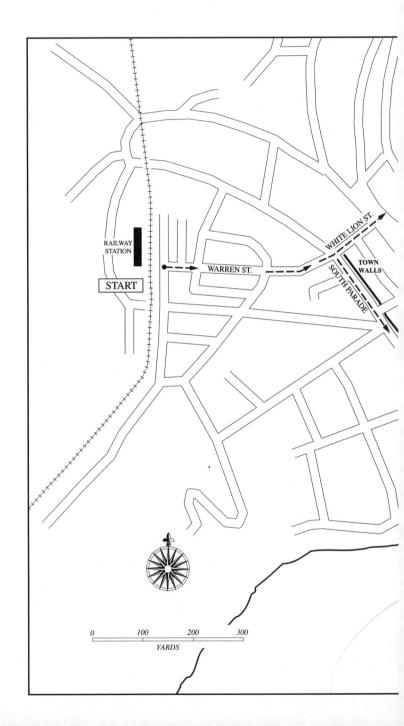

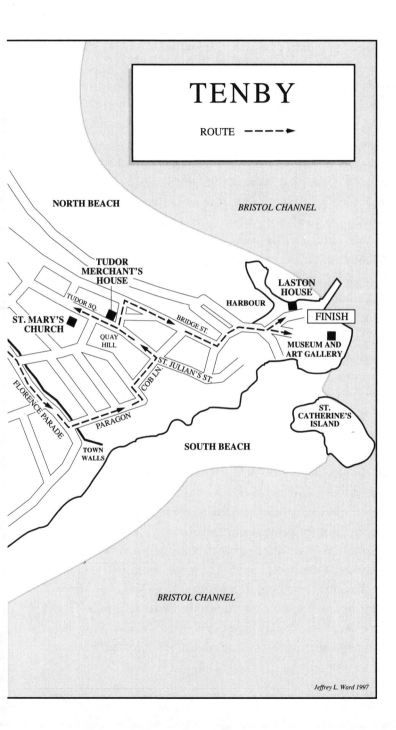

TENBY

ROUTE ----→

NORTH BEACH

BRISTOL CHANNEL

TUDOR MERCHANT'S HOUSE

LASTON HOUSE

HARBOUR

TUDOR SQ.

BRIDGE ST.

FINISH

ST. MARY'S CHURCH

QUAY HILL

MUSEUM AND ART GALLERY

ST. JULIAN'S ST.

COB LN.

FLORENCE PARADE

PARAGON

ST. CATHERINE'S ISLAND

TOWN WALLS

SOUTH BEACH

BRISTOL CHANNEL

Jeffrey L. Ward 1997

plunder and express their resentment. It was against the Welsh that the surviving medieval walls were built.

Tenby was besieged in the 1640s, but this time as part of the English civil war between Charles I and parliament. By the 1700s the prosperity which had once radiated from the medieval harbor was long gone. Tenby lay in ruins, its main gate battered by the cannons of the victorious parliamentary army, its houses roofless. There was a problem from pigs roaming the impoverished streets. But after the French revolution, with continental Europe closed to English aristocratic tourists, elegant eyes fell on this promising spot. The new fashion of sea bathing was well suited by the sheltered sands of Tenby. And the remoteness of the town kept away most of the ordinary folk. Tall, flat-fronted town houses in the Georgian and early Victorian styles were built on each side of the headland. Tenby, for knowing visitors, was reborn.

Tenby is best reached by train. (From London, you will normally need to change trains at Swansea.) From Tenby station walk a few hundred yards along **Warren Street.** Where South Parade runs in from the right, you see the beginnings of the long medieval town wall, stretching away to your right. Walk along it in a moment. But first, a view of the sea. Continue in the same direction as you walked from the station, along **White Lion Street** until you reach the road along the clifftop. Below you now stretches the **North Beach.** Its great isolated rock is Goscar Rock. The sea beyond is Carmarthen Bay. Across the bay in the distance and to the right you can see, in most weather, the great peninsula of the Gower.

Now that you have seen the fine beach below, you may want to go immediately down the steep steps to the sand. There will be other lovely beaches along your way. Go back down White Lion Street toward the town wall. On the way notice the **Royal Lion pub.** This was the site of the North Gate in the town wall. Here in 1644 the big guns of parliament broke through the gate and forced the royalists in Tenby to surrender. When you reach the surviving town wall, on the corner with South Parade again, turn left and walk alongside the wall, noticing the long vertical slits for reconnaissance and arrows. About one hundred yards along the wall is the first projecting tower. (Towers allowed defenders to direct arrows from the side, or even the rear, of attackers.) Your path leads under the tower. Also under the tower is an entry to the old town, but keep on to the next tower, where there are now six large entrances in the stonework. This was the West Gate. Look at the entrance which leads into the old town. In the stonework on the right of this entrance, about four feet from the ground, you will see various recesses designed to hold the original gate. Go in through this gateway, then turn and look back at traces of the walkway which once ran along the top of the walls.

Pass two more towers. This section of the wall was rebuilt to defend against a Spanish invasion force, the Armada of 1588. The wall ends in an arch by the entrance to the **Imperial Hotel.** (The Imperial is highly recommended. Many of the rooms have superb views, and the food meets the high standard of the French Routiers organization.) Before going through the arch, continue for thirty yards to see the view from the cliff. Ahead of you is Caldey; you can see the sandy beach where boats land, bringing supplies and visitors to the monastery. In the evening, the monks must look over from their dark island to the lights of Tenby, the cheerful, glittering town, and think of the world they reject.

Closer, to your left, is another island, St. Catherine's, with a large, grim building of stone. This was constructed as a fort in the 1860s, and heavily armed with cannons. Its purpose was to deter any French invasion force which might try to use the harbor of Tenby. Relations with France improved. In 1907 the fort was sold, and re-equipped as a flashy home by a rich family. Their larger items of shopping were hauled up the cliff by pulley. Also to your left, far across the sea, are the great cliffs at the end of the Gower peninsula, known as Worm's (meaning "Dragon's") Head.

Go back to the arch leading to the Imperial Hotel. Before going through, look up to the right of the arch at the battered remains of a nineteenth-century lamp—an oil lamp, we suspect. Walk past the front of the hotel and keep to the path nearest the sea. Forty yards past the hotel a pleasant clifftop garden opens on the right. "No dogs allowed" says a sign at the entrance. Reading between the lines we gather that the public is allowed. The street here is the **Paragon.** Just before it bends left, you may like to explore the steps which lead down to the beach—or to the waves at high tide. Follow the Paragon around its bend. Forty yards farther along turn right into Cob Lane, with its cottages from the 1700s.

Where **Cob Lane** reaches busy **St. Julian's Street,** turn left and walk to the entrance of the late medieval St. Mary's Church. Inside, to the right of the altar, is a statue from the 1630s of local merchant William Risam. The damage near its head is said to have been caused by the musket of a Puritan soldier in the conquering parliamentary army. For Puritans, statues in church suggested idolatry and Catholicism. Left of the altar are colorful alabaster statues from 1610 or a little later, showing local grandee Thomas ap Rees, his wife, and seven children ("ap" in Welsh is the equivalent of "Mc-" in Irish names). Husband and wife wear the neck ruffs fashionable in Shakespeare's day. He wears a rather theatrical suit of armor.

Back at the church entrance, turn right to retrace your route until you reach, on the left, an alley which goes downhill toward the harbor. This is **Quay Hill.** A few yards along the alley, on the left, is the **Plantagenet Restaurant,** known for excellent food in a delightful setting. In the adjoining basement is an associated, and similarly well run bar. Then, on the left, comes the **Tudor Merchant's House,** seemingly from the late 1400s. If it's open, go in to look at the massive stone fireplace, no doubt much appreciated by those with damp clothes in the days when travel was slow and mainly on foot—or in open boat. Winters in South Wales are famously wet. The ground floor of the house was probably used for trade; the family lived above.

Continue down Quay Hill toward the harbor. In the wall of the last building in the alley, on the right, look for the stone remains of an ancient door and window. Where Quay Hill ends, turn right into **Bridge Street** for a view of the harbor and of the elegant early nineteenth-century town houses in their pastel colors. As you go along Bridge Street, look out for the decorative metal fanlights above the doors of two adjoining houses. Where Bridge Street ends, go right for a moment into St. Julian's Street to see, on the left and set back a little from the road, a lovely terrace of fine buildings in the Georgian style, with inset columns crowned by ramhorn curls—Ionic volutes.

Now go back down St. Julian's Street, passing on your right the lanes which lead to Castle Beach and to the Tenby Museum, and on your left the road to the harbor. Ahead of you is a courtyard, **Castle Square.** Look for the grand entrance of **Laston House,** built in 1810. This building was at the heart of the successful plan to turn Tenby into a fashionable resort. Sir William Paxton, a London banker who saw Tenby's potential, created Laston House as a center for bathing, coffee-drinking, and for general stylish lounging, all at very high prices. There was, as with skiing today, the comforting thought that this activity led to health and fitness. Above the door of Laston House is a motto in Greek: ΘΑΛΑΣΣΑ ΚΛΥΖΕΙ ΠΑΝΤΑ ΤΑΝΘΡΩΠΩΝ ΚΑΚΑ (The sea washes away all human ills). This too was a mechanism for social exclusion, though a more delicate one than the high prices. In 1810, if you had the education to be comfortable with classical Greek, you were likely to be financially the sort Paxton was looking for. The Greek words may have an additional meaning here. In its original context, Euripides'

Iphigenia in Tauris, the phrase is used to claim that seawater is a better cure than spring water; for Paxton the great commercial rivals of Tenby were the inland spring health spas, such as Bath.

Walk back a few yards to the lane which leads uphill to the **Tenby Museum.** This little hill, the headland of Tenby, was the site of a Norman castle. As you enter the lane you pass through the old castle gateway. Look for the slots in the second archway on the left. These were for the portcullis, the hefty iron grid which dropped to bar the way to attackers.

Pass the museum for the footpath which leads to the top of the headland. On the summit is a stone watchtower, the only striking thing to survive of the medieval castle. If you would like to explore beyond the town, the view from here may help you to choose which of countless seaside walks to take. For the trip to Caldey, boats leave (at high tide) from the quay in the harbor and (at low tide) from Castle Beach—facing Caldey and just below you here. The season for these boats is usually from the week after Easter until October. At Caldey, the Cistercian monks sell the chocolate and perfume which they make. Visitors who walk beyond the monastery have the island largely to themselves. The sea is wilder here. On sunny days butterflies flourish.

Before you leave the headland, the museum and its art gallery deserve a visit. Pictures by Charles Norris show the ruins of old Tenby around 1800, before the town recovered its beauty. Above all, look for the work of Tenby's two most famous people: sister and brother, the early twentieth-century artists Gwen and Augustus John. Augustus's imposing physique, bohemian appearance, and wild lifestyle helped to make him internationally known. He said, however, that the work of his quieter sister, an associate of the sculptor Rodin, would one day be better appreciated than his own. The museum holds some thirty works by Augustus John, and six by Gwen. Look especially for Gwen's portrait of her sister, Winifred John.

In leaving Tenby, it's worth remembering Paxton and the other visionaries of the early 1800s who saw what the place could be and had the tenacity to carry out their plans. The town has also been managed with great tact and success in recent times. Augustus John's words about Tenby still come close: "You may travel the world over, but you will find nothing more beautiful. It is so restful, so colourful and so unspoilt."

Useful phone numbers:
Tourist Information office, Tenby: 01834 842402
Imperial Hotel: 01834 843737
Plantaganet Restaurant: 01834 842350

✤ WELLS

Wells is unique and captivating. It is the best-preserved and least-changed cathedral town in England. At the foot of the **Mendip hills** in the heart of Somerset, Wells has retained its tranquil old-world character. Here you will feel the atmosphere of a medieval town. Since the cathedral was not a monastic foundation, Wells's clerical institutions suffered less destruction than other cathedral cities. The combination of the walled, self-sufficient, ecclesiastical establishment and the small market town will give you a better idea of what a cathedral city must have been like several centuries ago than any other place in England.

Wells is a little more than half-an-hour's drive from Bath. Or if you are coming by bus, it will take about an hour to do the twenty miles.

The town derives its name from the springs which rise very close to the cathedral and have threatened it throughout the centuries.

Begin your stroll (for Wells is so minute and full of one interesting place next to the other that you will stroll slowly) in the old **Market Place** with its **stone courts** and **half-timbered buildings.** On market days vendors will be crying their wares from stalls where flowers, vegetables, and furniture will be on sale. There are several interesting shops around the square.

Look for the Crown Hotel, an inn from the 1400s. Here in 1695 the Quaker William Penn preached without permission from a second-story window to a great crowd below. He was arrested for this. The royalist authorities of the time were always nervous about Non-Conformist religion, which had been at the heart of the republican side in the civil wars of the 1640s.

After looking about the Market Place, approach the **cathedral** through **Penniless Porch,** where beggars sat in former days. The Porch, in reality a tall and attractive stone gatehouse, was built in the mid-1400s by a Bishop Bekynton. So was the other, and even finer, gatehouse just to the right—now known as the Bishop's Eye. A few yards to your left in the close the sight of the magnificent **west front** of the cathedral will burst upon you.

A church has stood near this site since King Ina of the West Saxons founded one about A.D. 704. The oldest part of the present cathedral dates from 1189 and the west front was consecrated in 1239. The cathedral with its central and western towers has stood very much as you see it today for almost five hundred years.

Before entering the cathedral, for the best view of its façade cross to the farthest point of the green in front of the building. Here you will find the ancient Brown's Gate. In this gatehouse is a tearoom with tables overlooking the green and cathedral—a good place to linger.

As you return across the green to the cathedral, the gray building on the left, with battlements and huge studded doors, is the Old Deanery, where Henry VII, father of Henry VIII, is recorded as having stayed in 1497.

Walk to the brownish-gray stone front of the cathedral. It is heavily weathered because Wells Cathedral gets the full force of any

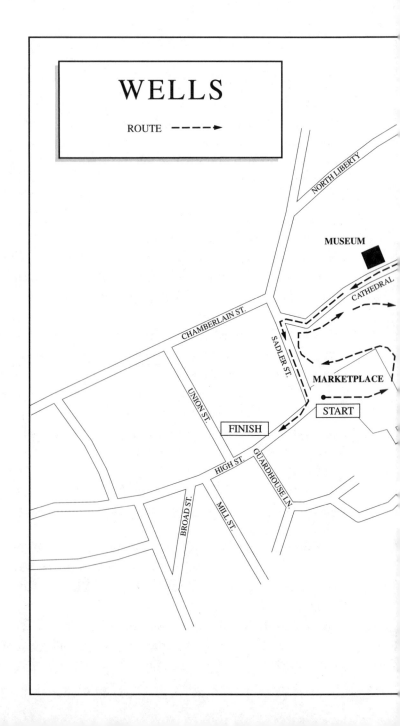

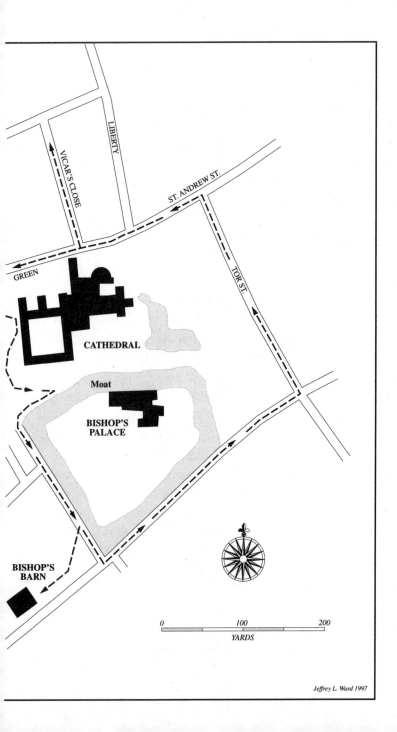

LIBERTY

VICAR'S CLOSE

ST. ANDREW ST.

GREEN

TOR ST.

CATHEDRAL

Moat

BISHOP'S
PALACE

BISHOP'S
BARN

0   100   200
YARDS

Jeffrey L. Ward 1997

storm from the Atlantic Ocean. There is no range of hills between the cathedral and the coast.

More than three hundred carved stone **statues** decorate this superb façade, which has often been compared to the cathedrals of Amiens and Rouen. This collection of figures is the finest group of medieval sculpture in the country. The front is unusual in another way for the entrance doors are quite small.

On entering the cathedral's **nave** with its graceful arches, the **inverted arch** beneath the central tower will at once catch your eye. These crossed arches were erected about 1330 to prevent the central tower from collapsing. Near these central arches, on each side of the altar, are two beautiful stone chapels—the **Sugar and Bubwith chantries** erected in the fifteenth century.

The **clock** in the north transept is one of the cathedral's most interesting sights. Since it has a face, and Salisbury Cathedral's old clock does not, this is said to be the oldest complete mechanical clock in England and reputedly dates from 1392, though the original mechanism, now in a museum, was replaced by the present one in the 1830s. Be sure to see the clock strike the hour. Then the great bell on the tower strikes, and the toy figures of knights on horseback circle in a joust, weapons clashing. On the quarter hour the figure of Jack Blandifer, above on the right, sounds the note by kicking his heels and two jacks in fifteenth-century armor perform on the outside of the cathedral. The interior clock face is beautifully designed and decorated to show the days of the month and phases of the moon as well as the time. Close to you now, behind a stone screen facing the clock, is the effigy and tomb of Bishop Still, head of two Cambridge colleges in the days of Elizabeth I. He is shown wearing an Elizabethan ruff round his neck.

Go through the pair of ancient doors which you can see from Still's tomb, and up the wonderful **flight of stairs,** well worn during the centuries, leading to the **Chapter House** completed by

1306. Note the exquisite vaulting in the spacious octagonal room. Cromwell's Puritan troops reportedly smashed the pictorial stained glass of the medieval windows here, as symbols of Catholicism and idolatry.

Stroll through the choir and look up at the great **east window,** dating from the early fourteenth century, in brilliant green and gold. While you are wandering about the nave and transepts, be sure to notice the beautifully carved **capitals** and little figures chiseled in the stone, remarkable examples of fine medieval sculpture.

Return to the door by which you entered the cathedral, but do not go through. Instead, turn to the left and go through the cathedral shop. On leaving the shop, turn left into the cloisters. Look through the arches for a fine view of the somewhat austere **southwest tower** which you can see from here independently of the west front.

A doorway from the right of the cloister opens into the grounds of the **Bishop's Palace.** Stroll toward the **moat** which runs around it. The deep color of a great copper beech contrasts with the reddish standstone walls of the palace. As you approach the gatehouse, you are likely to notice **swans** swimming about. They have been taught to ring a bell (which you will see below a window of the left gate tower) for more food after their daily feedings at 10:00 and 4:00.

The impressive brick palace dates from the thirteenth century and has been occupied by the Bishops of Bath and Wells ever since. The moat and battlemented wall were added a century later. They were to defend the then Bishop against his own townspeople, who had tried in vain to stop paying him rents. The grounds are open in summer on Tuesdays–Thursdays, between 10:00 and 6:00; on Sundays 2:00–6:00; and every day in August. They are closed in the winter. But if you stand on the inner side of the former drawbridge you can see to your left the large courtyard, the ruins of the Great Hall, and the battlemented towers.

In the Great Hall in 1539 the Abbot of nearby Glastonbury, Richard Whyting, was sentenced to death for obstructing Henry VIII's policy of seizing monastic property. He was taken from here to the prominent hill of Glastonbury Tor, where he was hung for a short time, then disembowelled and cut into pieces.

In the lovely **garden** of the palace there is a small pond fed by the seven deep springs or wells which give the town its name. The view of the cathedral's central tower rising above the lovely shrubbery and trees along the edge of the pond is one of the most beautiful in the close.

Turn left as you leave the drawbridge and wander past hawthorn trees along the wide **moat**—one of the most delightful walks in Wells. This is surely one of the widest and longest moats in England still to have its water. Now and again the cathedral tower is visible between the trees and above the **crenellated walls** that surround the Bishop's Palace. The ducks from the moat rest at times on top of these walls.

Just before this first long stretch of wall ends, turn right and cross the recreation ground. To the left of the bandstand is the Bishop's Barn, built in the 1400s to store the rents-in-kind paid to the bishops. These were obviously large; look at the size of the barn. Notice also the very narrow windows, designed to defeat medieval thieves.

Follow the moat around the palace. Where the moat and palace wall turn away from your path, look for the ornamental waterfall in the distance. Continue along the path, with great beech trees to your right, until you come to **Tor Street,** then turn left to **St. Andrew Street.** The back of the cathedral looms to your left. In a few moments you will pass **Liberty,** a street on your right. The Liberty was the area that was at one time under the sole control of the Dean and Chapter of the cathedral.

Just before you reach the stone archway, turn right into one of Wells's unique spots—**Vicars' Close,** reputed to be the most complete ancient street in Europe. Built in the fourteenth century, the

street and its uniform stone houses belong to the vicars of the cathedral. It remains substantially as it has been for six hundred years. Stroll along this row of houses with their tall chimneys and beautifully tended gardens. You will be enchanted by the little lawns and profusion of flowers—roses, fuchsia, hydrangea, and lavender. Notice how the close climbs to give an illusion of greater length. After walking to the lovely **chapel** at the end, return to the fourteenth-century **Vicars' Hall.**

On returning to St. Andrew Street, go back twenty yards to look at the lovely old cottage on the opposite side. (It is named "The Rib.") Notice the carving over the front door. In the side wall you can trace the ghosts of windows long bricked up, or rather, stoned up.

Now pass under the arch beside the cathedral. You will see the great face of the cathedral clock on your left. The **Wells Museum** (open daily, 10:00–5:30; closed Mondays and Tuesdays in winter) on your right, contains prehistoric and Iron Age relics of the nearby caves, Roman remains, natural history, and other specimens.

Continue along **Cathedral Green** to Brown's Gate. On the way you will pass a delightful garden at a vine-covered and turreted stone house, No. 6. Part of this canonical dwelling dates back to the thirteenth century. Go through the archway and past the ancient gatehouse whose recorded history goes back to 1580.

Once through the archway, go left into Sadler Street. When you reach the side of the Market Place once more, turn right into High Street and, on the right, look for the **Star pub.** With its cobbled lane, the archway leading into the pub yard preserves the atmosphere of a coaching inn. This is a lovely setting to relax at the end of your walk.

Useful phone number:
Tourist Information office, Wells: 01749 672552

⚜ YORK I

During the Middle Ages **York** was the second largest city in England—a position it held until the seventeenth century. Today as you stand in admiration before the world-renowned Minster, wander through York's narrow, irregular streets, or stroll along its ancient walls, you still feel the medieval influence. Despite the ever present reminders of the modern day, old York has succeeded in preserving its ancient character. Its Roman foundations, Norman fortress, medieval city walls and massive gateways, old churches, quaint houses, parks with ancient abbey ruins, and historic guildhalls will give you some sense of York's place in the stream of English history. York is full of interest, so don't make the mistake of thinking that the Minster and the Shambles—York's famous medieval street—are all that is worth seeing here.

York is a perfect city to wander in—you are almost bound to find yourself in an enchanting little street or an out-of-the-way corner with a delightful view of the Minster wherever you turn. If you saunter along the Lendal Bridge by the River Ouse, the effect of the buildings rising above the stream will make you think of cities on the Continent. A stroll along the walls will reveal delightful glimpses of old houses and charming gardens with the towers of the Minster as a dramatic backdrop. The most interesting old section of the city is in one rather small area so the places you want to see are close at hand.

York in northeast England is on the usual motor route up the east coast to Scotland. You can drive the approximately two hundred miles from London in a comfortable day's trip on double carriageways or expressways. By rail York is on the main line between London (less than three hours by fast train) and Edinburgh.

There is so much to see in York that two walks are suggested, each of which should take about half a day. Neither is long in distance. The first walk—quite short—ends at the Minster, so you will have plenty of time to enjoy this magnificent cathedral, the largest in England.

Start your first walk, if possible, fairly early in the morning, for on a clear day the light will be better at that hour to view the towers of the Minster from the walls. You should begin this tour at the entrance to the **Museum Gardens** on Museum Street one hundred yards from **Lendal Bridge.** Stroll into the pleasant park that runs down to the river. Go straight ahead and slightly uphill to the Doric columns of the **Yorkshire Museum** (open weekdays, 10:00–5:00). In addition to its fine exhibits of Roman remains, there are archeological, geological, and natural history collections as well as galleries of Saxon, Danish, and medieval antiquities. Don't miss the eighth-century silver-gilt Anglian **Ormside bowl.**

From the Museum walk a few yards farther to the ruins of **St. Mary's Abbey,** founded in 1089 and Yorkshire's first monastery after the Norman conquest. The gaunt shells of gothic windows stand amid pleasant lawns.

The most historic and best preserved bit of Roman York is the **Multangular Tower** on your left as you return to the park entrance

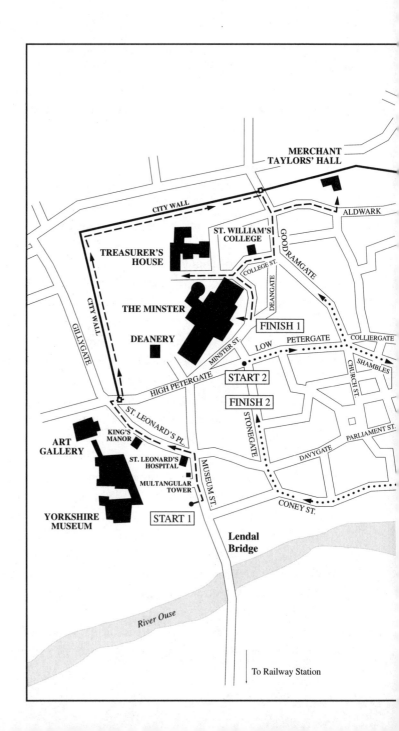

MERCHANT
TAYLORS' HALL

ALDWARK

CITY WALL

ST. WILLIAM'S
COLLEGE

TREASURER'S
HOUSE

COLLEGE ST.

GOODRAMGATE

CITY WALL

GILLYGATE

DEANGATE

THE MINSTER

DEANERY

FINISH 1

MINSTER ST.

LOW   PETERGATE   COLLIERGATE

START 2

SHAMBLES

HIGH PETERGATE

CHURCH ST.

FINISH 2

ST. LEONARD'S PL.

STONEGATE

ART
GALLERY

KING'S
MANOR

PARLIAMENT ST.

ST. LEONARD'S
HOSPITAL

MUSEUM ST.

DAVYGATE

MULTANGULAR
TOWER

YORKSHIRE
MUSEUM

START 1

CONEY ST.

Lendal
Bridge

River Ouse

To Railway Station

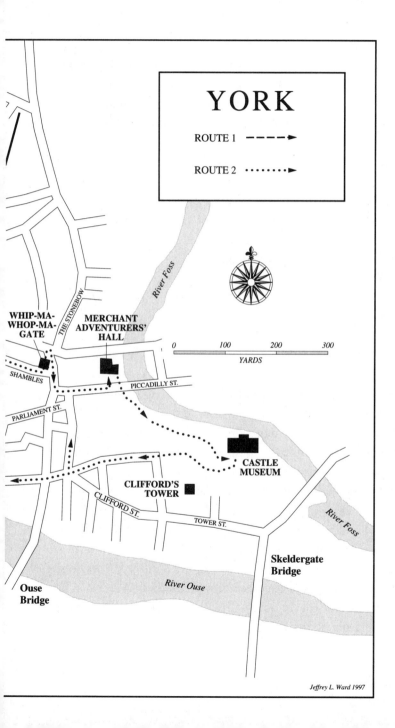

YORK

ROUTE 1 ----►

ROUTE 2 ••••••►

River Foss

0   100   200   300

YARDS

WHIP-MA-
WHOP-MA-
GATE

MERCHANT
ADVENTURERS'
HALL

THE STONEBOW

SHAMBLES

PICCADILLY ST.

PARLIAMENT ST.

CASTLE
MUSEUM

CLIFFORD'S
TOWER

CLIFFORD ST.

TOWER ST.

River Foss

Skeldergate
Bridge

Ouse
Bridge

River Ouse

Jeffrey L. Ward 1997

from the museum. This is one of the corner bastions of the Roman fortress and part of the early fourth-century **Roman wall** which is about four or five feet thick. The lower Roman section can be identified from the upper medieval wall by its smaller facing stones. Notice the layers of red tiles, a favorite Roman device for binding and strengthening walls.

Roman York dates from A.D. 71 when a fortress was established on the site of the present Minster. Known during the 340 years of Roman occupation as Eboracum, York was visited by the Emperors Hadrian and Severus and was the scene of the proclamation of Constantine the Great as Emperor.

At the end of the wall stand the thirteenth-century remains of **St. Leonard's Hospital** once, it is claimed, the biggest hospital in the north of England. It perished in 1540, when Henry VIII was dissolving the monasteries.

Turning left on Museum Street, you will pass the **Public Library** in a few yards. To the left of the library entrance you can get a closer look, away from crowds, at the Multangular Tower and Roman wall.

Now bear left on **St. Leonard's Place** past eighteenth-century houses with lovely railings and balconies. Almost opposite the **Theatre Royal** you will notice more remains of the Roman wall, a portion of the legionary fortress built in the fourth century. **King's Manor** on the left, behind a large courtyard and lawn, was originally (1280) the residence of the abbot of St. Mary's, then was converted to a Tudor palace, and now is part of the University of York. This delightful building is worth exploring. It is built of red brick and stone—the latter taken, no doubt, from nearby Roman or monastic sites. The Manor was the home of the Earl of Strafford, favorite of King Charles I. Strafford lived here from 1628 until 1640, when he had a date with the executioner—Charles having thrown him to the wolves, in an attempt to placate his own enemies in parliament. The king stayed here in 1633 and 1639. Look for Charles's **coat of arms** above the entrance, then go into the building to reach its courtyards, refreshingly quiet after the bustle of the streets outside. A few yards farther on the left is the **City Art Gallery** (open weekdays, 10:00–5:00; Sundays, 2:30–5:00), a collection with particular stress on the Italian and Dutch schools. Some of the modern paintings upstairs are interesting.

After this introduction to York, you now approach the city's **ramparts.** Before crossing the road to reach them, look for the stone gateway with a plaque as follows: "This gateway was broken through the Abbey wall July 1503 in honour of the Princess Margaret, daughter of Henry VII, who was the guest of the Lord Abbot of St. Mary's for two days of her journey to the North as the bride of James IV of Scotland." Margaret was sister of the future Henry VIII. Her marriage had grave consequences. From it Margaret's descendants Mary Queen of Scots and James I (James VI of Scotland) got their claim on the throne of England. The result was the disastrous Stuart dynasty, notable for the civil wars it provoked. Opposite the art gallery stands the solid bulk of battlemented **Bootham Bar,** the gate that led to the north from which direction came York's ancient and most dangerous enemies—the Scots.

Before you climb up the steps at Bootham Bar leading to the **walk around the wall,** notice the **portcullis** under the gateway. This stretch of the fourteenth-century wall is particularly delightful and the most enjoyable of all sections of the city's walls. The walk is wide and made attractive by trees and flowering shrubs. While you stroll along, you have lovely views of the Minster's towers above the old roofs. From this vantage point, a tranquil air seems to settle over the city. You are removed from all the noise of traffic and left alone to contemplate the beauty of the charming gardens, old houses, and the majestic Minster. You can hear birdsong, a rare thing in a city center. On your right, the large brick house and lovely garden belong to **the Deanery.** On your left, after you turn the corner, you will see the remains of the **moat.**

Descend at **Monk Bar,** which was erected on Roman foundations about 1230–1250. Just before you descend, the gatehouse contains a pleasant little **museum.** There is a working **portcullis** and an audio "trial" of the (Yorkist) King Richard III, on the charge of murdering his dynastic rivals the little "Princes in the Tower (of London)." At ground level, go through the gate to look up at its grim and lofty **turrets** from outside, as an attacker would have seen them. The gate was designed to be menacing, and it succeeds. A few steps from Monk Bar on **Goodramgate** turn left on **Aldwark** and walk one hundred yards to visit the **Merchant Taylors' Hall.** This late fourteenth-century hall became in 1415 the property of the Craft of Tailors, one of York's earliest city guilds. Its spacious hall, set back behind a broad lawn, has a remarkably fine late fourteenth-century timber roof.

Retrace your steps to Goodramgate, turn left and shortly go right on curved **College Street.** On your right is **St. William's College**—now an information center for visitors to the Minster. A black and white Tudor building with overhanging story, it was established in the 1460s for the cathedral's chantry priests. In this building Charles I had printing presses for his propaganda early in the civil war. He had moved his court to York in 1642, London being dominated by his enemies, the parliament. Notice the fine wood carving of the restored outer doorway. If you look carefully you will find a little figure of a mouse, the trademark of a prominent contemporary wood carver, in the upper corner of the outside door. Go into the cobbled inner quadrangle, which is early Georgian. You can also see interesting seventeenth-century stairs and an open timber roof in the principal chamber.

Continue past St. William's College and keep right into **Minster Yard** behind the cathedral. Turn right again into a **cobbled lane** (which follows the line of a Roman road) and pass cottages to reach on your left the entrance to the Treasurer's House. The bracket of an eighteenth-century oil lamp projects above the door. The **Treasurer's House** is open 10:30–5:30, daily. Built originally at the end of the eleventh century on the site of the Roman barracks, the house as it stands today is mainly post-seventeenth century. It is a most beautifully proportioned building and has been tastefully furnished with fine period furniture and works of art. Now owned by the National Trust, it is well worth visiting, especially for those who admire seventeenth- and eighteenth-century furniture and interior decoration. The grounds are also most attractive. Cross the walled garden and leave by the gate. Set in the garden wall, outside, is a plaque recording a moving piece of history: "From a window in the Treasurer's House . . . the young deaf and dumb astronomer John Goodricke, 1764–86, . . . observed the periodicity of the star Algol and discovered the variation of δ Cephei and other stars, thus laying the foundation of modern measurement of the Universe."

Walk to the right around the Minster to view this most spectacular cathedral from its splendid **west front.** The present structure, begun about 1220, is the fifth cathedral to be built on this site. King Edwin of Northumbria put up a wooden chapel and was baptized here in 627. Pause for a few moments to study the superb stonework of the portals and the entire magnificent **façade,** one of the finest in all Europe.

When you enter, the vastness of the Minster's interior will impress you at once. But York's outstanding characteristic is its treasure of medieval **stained glass,** unequaled in England. Turn back to view the great **west window** with its amazingly beautiful flamboyant tracery. When you reach a point beneath the central tower, look to your left in the north transept at York's most famous glass windows, **the Five Sisters.** These are the largest lancet windows in the world. Their grisaille (grayish green) glass is thirteenth century and is said to consist of 100,000 separate pieces. York Minster's extraordinary collection of medieval glass is a treasure unrivaled in England and renowned throughout the world.

To the right of the north transept you will find the **Chapter House,** a very beautifully proportioned original chamber and considered one of the finest in the country. Its **pyramidal roof** is unique and its windows have been restored with their original glass. The Saxon Book of the Gospels and Horn of Ulphus are among the treasures on exhibit.

Return to the north transept, then turn left along the north choir aisle. Go in the choir to see the new choir stalls. As you stroll around the choir, you will admire two huge **windows** (St. William and St. Cuthbert) with the world's finest fifteenth-century glass. The largest area of stained glass ever made is the early fifteenth-century **east window** above the Lady Chapel. Seventy-six feet high and thirty-two feet broad, it contains more than two thousand square feet of medieval glass.

Before you leave this glorious cathedral, pause once again beneath the central tower and have a final look at these marvelous stained-glass windows. Their beauty and the vast proportions of the Minster will leave you with a profound sense of humility and awe for the artistry of the Middle Ages.

York II ⚜

This second walk will take you through York's quaint, narrow streets with their old houses and overhanging second stories. In no other large English city have the streets and buildings of medieval days been more successfully preserved on such an extensive scale. Though you will be strolling through the heart of a modern city, at every hand you will find much to remind you of York as it was hundreds of years ago.

Start at the **Church of St. Michael-le-Belfry,** forty yards from the entrance of the Minster. Here Guy Fawkes, who attempted to blow up the Houses of Parliament, was baptized in 1570. After admiring the church's fine **stained glass,** go out into **High Petergate** and turn left. At the junction of **Stonegate** only a few feet away, note the decorative figure over the corner of the brick building, a Minerva in Georgian dress, from 1801. Just opposite you can see "1646" carved on the corner pillar. Continue along **Low Petergate,** built over a Roman road and so named since the thirteenth century, past enticing gift shops. (The element "gate" at the end of street names in York does not mean "gate" in our sense. York for a time was a Viking city, and in the Norse language "gata" meant "street.") Look back for a dramatic view of the Minster's Towers rising above the peaked and tiled roofs.

Turn left at Goodramgate and go for about fifty yards to a gate on the left leading to the odd little church of **Holy Trinity** in the midst of an ancient **churchyard.** Some of the houses on your right are among the oldest in York. Although the foundations of Holy Trinity date from the thirteenth century, the present building is about a hundred years later. You will be interested in the church's uneven flooring, its seventeenth-century "box" pews, and its lovely east window (1472). This is an austere but delightful place.

Return to the junction of Low Petergate and Goodramgate, then bear left into flagstoned **Kings Square.** Leave the square by the exit on the right. By the old corner building whose upper story rests on wooden beams taken from Elizabethan ships, you come to the famous **Shambles.** Just before you stroll into the Shambles, turn right into **King's Court** to an open-air food and clothing market once called "Coney Garth" (rabbit garden).

Once the street of the butchers, the Shambles takes its name from the stalls on which meat used to be displayed. This fascinating, tiny street—barely wide enough for one cart—was mentioned in the Domesday Book, and assumed its present character about 1400. The overhanging upper stories of the timbered houses with their steep gables come so close together that at one point a person could almost lean out the window and shake hands with a neighbor across the street. Nowadays antique and curio shops, jewelers, silver-smiths, woodcraftsmen, and other fine stores have made the Shambles rather fashionable. The fifteenth-century hall of the **Butchers' Guild** is upstairs at Nos. 41–42 on your right. At No. 37 go into an alley to look at this house's ancient timbers.

At the end of the Shambles, go left down a narrow passageway to the **Whip-Ma-Whop-Ma-Gate,** York's shortest street. Seemingly the name derives from an ancient joke: the spelling "Whitnourwhatnourgate" is recorded from 1505, meaning "no idea what kind of street," "what a street"!

Turn right along **Pavement** where once a gallows stood and go left at the busy intersection on **Piccadilly** to the historic **Merchant Adventurers' Hall** set back in a lawn below the street level (open daily, 9:00–5:00). This black and white timbered building, probably the finest medieval guild hall in York, was built in the mid-fourteenth century by the company of mercers who became the Merchant Adventurers a century later. This company, once the most powerful in York, still exists as a charitable organization. The **great hall,** with its elegant high-pitched roof used to be the place where cloth, that the weavers had made on handlooms at home, was brought for trading and for export. Be sure to visit the ancient **undercroft** with its fourteenth-century windows. It used to be divided into cubicles for the guild's pensioners, "poor and feeble persons," until Victorian times. The oldest part is the wall along the garden. The company's records for purchase of bricks and stone in 1358 show that twenty thousand handmade bricks were bought for seven pence a thousand, which was considered expensive. However, stone at fourteen pence a ton was relatively cheap.

Go back into Piccadilly. Cross the street. Walk a few yards to the left, to the bridge over the **River Foss.** Turn right, onto the **riverside path** which will bring you within sight of **Clifford's Tower.** The tower stands on top of a mound which William the Conqueror constructed as a fortress. The remains of the existing stone tower, built in quatrefoil plan, date from the thirteenth century. If you care to climb a long flight of steps, you can walk along its walls. From outside you see that the walls lean outward, making the visitors walking along the top appear to be in a rather precarious position.

Just beyond Clifford's Tower you will see the **Castle Museum** (open weekdays, 9:30–8:00, Sundays, 10:00–8:00; from October to March, closes at 5:00). Although various sections of this folk museum are of considerable interest, the most remarkable and lifelike parts are **Alderman's Walk** and **Kirkgate.** These are reconstructed streets, together with fronts of houses and shops, exactly as they were in Victorian and Edwardian York. In fact, the cobbled street, with its old lampposts and hansom cab, the lighted shops and their windows full of goods which were popular during those days are so realistic that you can hardly believe you have not been transported to York of a century ago. The detail of the buildings and their contents has been so faithfully executed that you will certainly find this living museum to be one of the most fascinating experiences in York and perhaps in your tour of England. The old firehouse, post office, cordwainer, saddles, book shop, and confectionery are all so enticing that you will find one more interesting than the next. The Victorian parlor of 1880 is particularly nostalgic. You can even wander in some of the shops and inspect what your ancestors used to buy.

Before you leave the museum, you may want to see upstairs the attractive **period rooms** of Jacobean, Georgian, and Victorian days.

The adjoining building, an extension of the museum, was formerly the Debtors' Prison. Here you can see on the ground floor a series of **craft workshops** such as a comb and clay pipe maker, tanner, printer, gunsmith, blacksmith, etc. On the first floor there is a display of eighteenth- and nineteenth-century **costumes.** Don't miss the **toy collection** and doll house which children will find delightful.

Retrace your steps, keeping Clifford's Tower on your left, and head for the church steeple. On reaching the church, in **Castlegate,** turn right down a slope into **Coppergate.** You may see a line of people waiting to enter York's most famous modern attraction—the **Yorvik Viking Centre.** This is a dramatic and successful re-enactment of daily life of the city (called "Jorvik" in Norse) while under Viking rule, before the Norman conquest. Not just the sights but the sounds and smells of the Norse town are re-created.

From the Viking Centre retrace your steps up the slope of Coppergate, turn right into Castlegate. At the road junction, go straight ahead along first the short Nessgate then pedestrian Spurriergate. The **Church of Martin Le Grand** on the left-hand side possesses very fine medieval glass. Walk along Spurriergate and on into **Coney Street.** When you reach **St. Helen's Square** you will see on your left the stately early eighteenth-century **Mansion House** where the Lord Mayor lives. Just behind the Mansion House down a passageway is York's restored **Guildhall** with a fine timbered roof.

Stroll through St. Helen's Square and just opposite the Mansion House you will enter **Stonegate,** an ancient street known to have existed in the twelfth century. When you stand at the entrance of Stonegate and look along this charming old street, you will notice how many different building styles from the fifteenth century on can be seen on either side of this single street. In the eighteenth century, coffee houses lined the street. Now its shop fronts with their bay windows retain its character. Halfway along is the fifteenth-century **Mulberry Hall** with its overhanging second-story bay windows, which are leaded with diamond-shaped panes.

In a few yards you will come to the sign of **Ye Olde Starre Inn,** one of the few inn-signs in England built across the street. Turn left down an alley to visit this colorful pub. Its yard is a welcome, peaceful place for a drink. On returning to Stonegate, you may wish to finish this interesting walk through old York by browsing about the many delightful shops on either side of this street and then to top it off, stroll a few yards beyond the end of Stonegate for a final look at the Minster, to which you will always return while visiting York.

Phone: Tourist Information, York: 01904 621756

Index

Adam, Robert, 6
Alfred House, 14
All Souls College
    (Oxford), 101
Anchor pub, 34
André, Major John, 13
Antelope Inn, 71–72
Archbishop's palace, 46
Armstrong, Major Henry,
    81
art galleries and museums
    Cambridge, 36
    Chichester, 54
    Knole House, 92, 93
    Tenby, 148–49
    York, 163
art in public places
    Cambridge, 21, 22, 23,
        32–33
    Canterbury, 45
    Chichester, 51–52
    Church Stretton, 64–65
    Oxford, 103, 110, 111
    Salisbury, 128, 130

Wells, 154
York, 165–66
Astley, Sir Jacob, 136
Audley House, 130
Austen, Jane, 10–11

Baccelli, Giannetta, 91,
    92
Bacon, Francis, 22
Bath
    Abbey Green, 7
    Alfred Street, 14
    Bartlett Street, 14
    Bath Street, 9
    Bennett Street, 13
    bridges, 6, 15
    Brock Street, 13
    churches, 6, 7–8
    Church Street, 7
    the Circus, 13
    Cross Bath, 9–10
    first walk, 3, 6–11
    gardens, 6, 13, 16
    Gay Street, 12

George Street, 12
High Street, 15
history of, 3, 6
hospitals, 15
houses of historic
    interest, 6–7, 10–11,
    12, 13, 14
Lilliput Alley, 7
maps of, 4, 5
Margaret's Buildings,
    13
Miles's Buildings, 12
Milsom Street, 14
museums, 14
New Bond Street, 15
Old Bond Street, 15
Old King Street, 12
Old Orchard Street, 7
Pierrepont Street, 6–7
pubs, 8, 15
Queen Square, 10
Queen Street, 10
Quiet Street, 10
restaurants, 10, 12

Bath (cont'd)
  Roman artifacts, 8, 9–10
  second walk, 12–16
  Shires Yard, 14–15
  theaters, 7
  transportation to, 6
  Trim Street, 10
  Upper Borough Walls, 10
Bath Abbey, 6, 7–8
Bath Assembly Rooms, 13–14
Bath City Markets, 15
Bath Theatre, 7
beaches, 144
Bear Inn, 111
Beaufort, Lady Margaret, 27, 28
Becket, Archbishop Thomas, 40, 41, 45, 47
Bell Harry Tower, 44
bell towers, 51
Bishop's Palace (Chichester), 52
Bishop's Palace (St. David's), 114, 116–17
Bishop's Palace (Wells), 155–56
Blackman House, 53
Black Prince, 45
Blue Boar pub, 84
Bodleian Library, 100
Boleyn, Anne, 92
bookstores, 77, 81, 83, 84
Booth, Richard, 80
Bootham Bar, 163
Bourchier, Archbishop Thomas, 88
Brasenose College (Oxford), 101
Bridge of Sighs, 25
bridges
  Bath, 6, 15

Cambridge, 23, 25, 26–27, 32, 33, 34
  Oxford, 101–2
Buck's Head pub, 63
"bumps" races, 104
Burke, Edmund, 6
Butchers' Guild, 168
Byron, George Gordon, Lord, 22

Caldey island, 141, 145, 148
Cambrian pub, 121
Cambridge
  All Saints' Passage, 27
  art galleries and museums, 36
  art in public places, 21, 22, 23, 32–33
  the Avenue, 23, 24
  Benson Court, 25
  bridges, 23, 25, 26–27, 32, 33, 34
  Bridge Street, 27
  Castle Street, 25
  Christ's College, 28
  churches, 21, 23, 27, 29, 32–33, 35, 36
  Clare College, 33
  clock towers, 21, 31
  cloisters, 34–35
  Corpus Christi College, 35
  first walk, 17, 20–28
  gardens, 23, 26, 28, 33, 36
  Garret Hostel Lane, 32
  Gonville and Caius College, 30, 31
  graffiti, 31
  Great Court, 21
  history of, 17, 20
  King's College, 17, 29
  King's Parade, 29
  libraries, 23, 26, 31

  Magdalene College, 22, 25, 26
  Magdalene Street, 25
  maps of, 18, 19
  museums, 25
  Northampton Street, 24
  Old Court, 35
  Pembroke College, 35
  Pembroke Street, 35
  Peterhouse College, 36
  pubs, 24, 26, 34
  Queens' College, 34–35
  Queens' Road, 34
  roofscapes, 21
  St. Catherine's College, 35
  St. John's College, 24, 25, 27
  second walk, 29–36
  Senate House, 30–31
  Sidney Sussex College, 27–28
  Silver Street, 34
  tourist information, 36
  transportation to, 20
  Trinity College, 20–23
  Trinity Lane, 32
  Trinity Street, 20–21
  Trumpington Street, 35
Cambridge Folk Museum, 25
Canterbury, 37–47
  art in public places, 45
  Butchery Lane, 43
  Butter Market, 44
  churches, 42–43, 44–46
  cloisters, 45–46
  gardens, 42
  Guildhall Street, 46
  High Street, 43
  history of, 37
  hospitals, 43

hotels, 40, 46
houses of historic
    interest, 42, 43
map of, 38–39
museums, 41, 43–44,
    46–47
pubs, 46
Roman artifacts, 43–44
St. Peter's Lane, 42
Stour Street, 46
Sun Street, 46
tourist information, 47
transportation to, 37
Westgate, 40
Canterbury Cathedral,
    44–46
Canterbury Heritage
    Museum, 46–47
Castle Museum, 170
castles
    Hay-on-Wye, 83–84,
        85
    St. David's, 114, 116–
        17
    Tenby, 148
    Wells, 155–56
Caxton, William, 129
Celts, 75–76
Chantry, 53
Chapter House (Canter-
    bury), 46
Chapter House (Salis-
    bury), 129–30
Chariots of Fire (film), 21
Charles, Prince, 22
Charles I, King, 28, 110,
    111, 136–37, 162–
    63, 164
Charles II, King, 26, 92,
    93
Chichester, 48–57
    art galleries and
        museums, 54
    art in public places,
        51–52
    Baffin's Lane, 54

bell towers, 51
Butter Market, 56
Canon Lane, 52
churches, 49, 51–52
East Street, 53, 54
gardens, 52–53, 54
Guildhall Street, 55
history of, 48
hospitals, 57
hotels, 49, 55–56, 57
houses of historic
    interest, 52, 53–54
Lion Street, 56–57
Little London, 54
map of, 50
Market Cross, 49
museums, 54–55
the Pallants, 53–54
Priory Road, 55
pubs, 57
restaurants, 52, 53
Roman artifacts, 49,
    51, 56
St. Martin's Square, 57
St. Martin's Street, 57
St. Richard's Walk, 52
South Street, 53
theaters, 56
tourist information, 57
Vicars' Close, 53
West Street, 49
Chichester Festival
    Theatre, 56
Christ Church Cathe-
    dral, 110
Christ Church College
    (Oxford), 108, 109–
    11
Christchurch Gate, 44
Christ Church Meadow,
    111
Christ's College (Cam-
    bridge), 28
Chubb's Alms House, 75
churches
    Bath, 6, 7–8

Cambridge, 21, 23, 27,
    29, 32–33, 35, 36
Canterbury, 42–43,
    44–46
Chichester, 49, 51–52
Church Stretton, 64–
    65
Dorchester, 72
Oxford, 102–3, 104,
    110
St. David's, 118
Salisbury, 124, 125,
    128–30, 131
Solva, 120
Stow-on-the-Wold,
    136, 139–40
Tenby, 146
Wells, 151, 154–55
York, 165–66, 167,
    168, 171
Church of Martin Le
    Grand, 171
Church of St. Michael-
    le-Belfry, 167
Church Stretton, 58–66
    art in public places,
        64–65
    Burway Road, 59
    churches, 64–65
    Church Street, 62, 64
    Church Way, 62
    Cunnery Road, 64
    Easthope Road, 59
    gardens, 63
    High Street, 62–63
    history of, 58–59
    houses of historic
        interest, 62, 64
    Longhills Road, 59
    map of, 60–61
    mountain climbing,
        65–66
    pubs, 63
    Sandford Avenue, 59
    tourist information, 64
    transportation to, 59

City Art Gallery (York), 163
City Museum (Chichester), 54–55
civil wars of mid-1600s, 136–37
Clare Bridge, 33
Clare College (Cambridge), 33
Clarendon building, 98–99
Clifford's Tower, 169–70
Clive, Lord, 13
clock towers
Cambridge, 21, 31
Hay-on-Wye, 80
Oxford, 105, 108, 109
Wells, 154
Cloister Court, 34–35
cloisters
Cambridge, 34–35
Canterbury, 45–46
Oxford, 102
Salisbury, 130
Coast path, 122–23
Cogidubnus, 48, 56
colleges and universities. See Cambridge; Oxford
Convocation House, 100
Corn Exchange, 54
Corpus Christi College (Cambridge), 35
Corpus Christi College (Oxford), 109, 111
Council House, 56
Cranmer, Archbishop Thomas, 88
Cromwell, Oliver, 27–28
Crown Hotel, 151

D. and B. Dickinson (shop), 15
Darwin, Charles, 28
David, St., 114

Deanery, The (Chichester), 52
Deanery, the (Oxford), 110
Deanery, the (York), 164
Dickens, Charles, 15, 46, 138
Dodgson, Charles (Lewis Carroll), 109, 110
Dolphin and Anchor Hotel, 49
Dorchester, 67–76
churches, 72
Colliton Street, 74
Cornhill Street, 71
Glyde Path Road, 74
Grey School Passage, 74
High East Street, 72
hotels, 72
houses of historic interest, 71, 74
Maiden Castle Lane, 75
map of, 68–69
museums, 72
prehistoric earthworks, 70–71, 75–76
restaurants, 72, 73
South Street, 71
tourist information, 76
transportation to, 70
Weymouth Avenue, 70
Dorchester Prison, 75
Dorset County Museum, 72
Drawda Hall, 106
Dudley, John, 88
Duke Humfrey's Library, 100

Edward III, King, 21
Edward VI, King, 51
Edwin of Northumbria, King, 165
Eisenhower, Dwight D., 55–56

Eleanor Bell, 139
El Greco, 103
Elizabeth I, Queen, 43, 110
English, Athene, 84
Erasmus building, 35
Exhibition Room, 100–101

Falstaff Hotel, 40
Fawkes, Guy, 167
fire brigades, 11
Fishbourne, 48
Fitzwilliam Museum, 36
Five Sisters (stained glass windows), 165–66
flint building, 52
Fosse Way, 133
Friary Hill, 75
furniture collections, 87, 92, 93–94

Gainsborough, Thomas, 13, 92, 110
gardens
Bath, 6, 13, 16
Cambridge, 23, 26, 28, 33, 36
Canterbury, 42
Chichester, 52–53, 54
Church Stretton, 63
Oxford, 103, 106
Tenby, 146
Wells, 156
York, 159
Gate of Honour, 31
Gate of Humility, 31
Gate of Virtue, 31
Gibbons, Grinling, 23
Gibbs Building, 29
Gloucester, Duke of, 22
Glyndwr, Owain, 83
Goldsmith, Oliver, 93
Gonville and Caius College (Cambridge), 30, 31

Goodricke, John, 165
Goscar Rock, 144
Gower, Bishop Henry
    de, 114, 118
Gower peninsula, 144,
    146
Grey, Jane, 88, 128
Grey, Lady Katherine,
    128–29
Grey Friars Friary, 47
Guildhall (Bath), 15–16
Guildhall (Chichester), 55
Guildhall (York), 171
Gwynne, Nell, 93

Hall, the (Cambridge), 22
Hamilton, Lady Emma, 7
Hangman's Cottage, 74
Harbour House Pub,
    118, 121
Hardy, Thomas, 67, 70,
    71, 72
Harnham Mill, 132
Harvey, William, 129
Haunch of Venison Inn,
    131
Hawksmoor, Nicholas,
    99, 105
Hay-on-Wye, 77–85
    Back Fold, 83–84
    bookstores, 77, 81, 83,
        84
    Bridge Street, 82
    Broad Street, 80–82
    Butter Market, 83
    castles, 83–84, 85
    Castle Street, 83, 84
    clock towers, 80
    hotels, 85
    houses of historic
        interest, 82
    leather shops, 84
    Lion Street, 82
    map of, 78–79
    pubs, 82, 84
    riverside walk, 85

    tourist information, 85
    transportation to, 80
Heath, Edward, 130
Henry I, King, 55
Henry II, King, 40
Henry VI, King, 32
Henry VII, King, 151
Henry VIII, King, 22,
    41, 110, 116
    Knole House and, 86,
        88, 91–92
Hertford College bridge,
    101–2
Holbein, Hans, the
    Younger, 22
Hole-in-the-Wall
    (restaurant), 12
Holy Trinity Church, 168
Honesty Bookshop, 83
hospitals
    Bath, 15
    Canterbury, 43
    Chichester, 57
    York, 162
hotels
    Canterbury, 40, 46
    Chichester, 49, 55–56,
        57
    Dorchester, 72
    Hay-on-Wye, 85
    St. David's, 118, 123
    Stow-on-the-Wold,
        137–38, 140
    Tenby, 145, 149
houses of historic interest
    Bath, 6–7, 10–11, 12,
        13, 14
    Canterbury, 42, 43
    Chichester, 52, 53–54
    Church Stretton, 62,
        64
    Dorchester, 71, 74
    Hay-on-Wye, 82
    Salisbury, 130–31
    Stow-on-the-Wold,
        136, 138, 139

    Tenby, 146–48
    York, 162–63, 165,
        168, 171
    see also Knole House
Housman, A. E., 58, 59

Imperial Hotel, 145, 149
Insurance House, 63

James I, King, 100, 111
James II, King, 10, 73, 93
Jeffreys, Judge George,
    73
John, Gwen and Augus-
    tus, 148–49
Johnson, Dr., 93

King's Arms Hotel (Dor-
    chester), 72
King's Arms Hotel (Stow-
    on-the-Wold), 137
King's Arms pub, 63
King's College (Cam-
    bridge), 17, 29
King's College Chapel,
    29, 32–33
King's Manor, 162–63
Knole House, 86–94
    Ballroom, 93
    Billiard Room, 93
    Bourchier's gatehouse,
        91
    Brown Gallery, 92
    café and rest rooms, 94
    Cartoon Gallery, 93
    furniture collection,
        87, 92, 93–94
    great gatehouse, 88
    Great Hall, 91–92
    Great Staircase, 92
    Green Court, 91
    guidebook to, 88
    King's Closet, 94
    King's Room, 93–94
    Leicester Gallery, 93
    maps of, 89, 90

Knole House (*cont'd*)
  opening and closing
    times, 87
  Reynolds Room, 93
  Shelley's Tower, 91
  Spangle Bedroom, 92
  Stone Court, 91
  tourist information, 94
  transportation to, 87
  Venetian Ambassador's
    Room, 93
Knole Park, 87, 94

Lanfranc, Archbishop, 44
Laston House, 147–48
Lawrence, Sir Thomas,
  110
leather shops, 84
libraries
  Cambridge, 23, 26, 31
  Oxford, 100, 104, 105,
    111
  York, 162
Liddell, Alice, 109, 110
lighthouses, 121–22
Locke, John, 110
Long Mynd, 58, 65–66
Lords of the Manor, 139
Loveless, George, 73
Lunatic Asylum for
  Gentlemen, 64

Magdalen College
  (Oxford), 106
Magdalene Bridge, 26–
  27
Magdalene College (Cam-
  bridge), 22, 25, 26
Magdalen Tower, 103
Magna Carta, 129
Maiden Castle, 75–76
Mansion House, 171
Mary I, Queen, 88
Mary II, Queen, 10
Mary of Modena, 9

Mathematical Bridge, 34
Maumbury Rings, 70–71
Mayor of Casterbridge,
  The (Hardy), 67, 70
Mendip hills, 150
Menkes, Suzy, 26–27
Merchant Adventurers'
  Hall, 169
Merchant Taylors' Hall,
  164
Merton College (Ox-
  ford), 108–9
Merton Corner, 22
Methodist church, 42–43
Mill pub, 34
mills, 132
Milton, John, 23, 28
Minster, the (York),
  165–66
Minstrels Gallery, 22
Mompesson House, 131
monasteries, 148
Monk Bar, 164
Monmouth, Duke of, 73
Montacute, Sir John de,
  128
Montgomery family, 55
Morgan, Timothy Guy,
  32
mountain climbing, 65–
  66
mounting steps, 82
Mulberry Hall, 171
Multangular Tower, 159,
  162
Museum Gardens, 159
Museum of Costume, 14
museums
  in Bath, 14
  in Cambridge, 25
  in Canterbury, 41, 43–
    44, 46–47
  in Chichester, 54–55
  clothing, 14
  craft workshops, 170

in Dorchester, 72
  folk life, 25
  history, 46–47, 54–55,
    72, 129–30, 157, 159
  living museums, 170
  prisons, 41
  Roman artifacts, 43–44
  in Salisbury, 129–30
  in Wells, 157
  in York, 159, 164, 170
  see also art galleries
    and museums

Napper's Mite, 71
Nash, Beau, 3, 8, 10
Nash, John, 56
Nelson, Lord, 6–7
Nevile, Thomas, 21
Nevile's Court, 22
New College (Oxford),
  102–3
New College Chapel,
  102–3
New College Garden,
  103
Newton, Sir Isaac, 21, 23
Non-Conformist chapel,
  120
Norris, Charles, 148
North, Roger, 23
Northanger Abbey
  (Austen), 11
North Beach, 144
North Canonry, 130
North Parade Bridge, 6
Nun's Garden, 106

Old Cross hotel, 118, 123
Old Mill pub, 132
Oliver Twist (Dickens),
  138
Olivier, Sir Laurence, 56
Oriel College (Oxford),
  111
Ormside bowl, 159

Orwell, George, 43
Oxford
    All Souls College, 101
    art in public places,
        103, 110, 111
    Brasenose College, 101
    bridges, 101–2
    Broad Street, 98
    Catte Street, 98
    Christ Church Col-
        lege, 108, 109–11
    churches, 102–3, 104,
        110
    clock towers, 105,
        108, 109
    cloisters, 102
    Convocation House,
        100
    Corpus Christi Col-
        lege, 109, 111
    covered market, 111–
        12
    Divinity School, 100
    Exhibition Room, 100–
        101
    first walk, 95, 98–107
    gardens, 103, 106
    Great Hall, 110
    Great Staircase, 110
    ilex tree, 102
    libraries, 100, 104,
        105, 111
    Magdalen College, 106
    map of, 96–97
    Merton College, 108–9
    New College, 102–3
    New College Lane,
        101
    Oriel College, 111
    pubs, 111
    punting, 106–7
    Queen's College, 103,
        105–6
    Radcliffe Camera, 99
    Rose Lane, 108
    St. Edmund Hall, 103–
        4
    second walk, 108–12
    theaters, 99
    Tom Quad, 109–10
    transportation to, 98
    Turf tavern, 102
    yew trees, 104–5

Pallant House, 54
Parade Gardens, 16
Paxton, Sir William, 147
Pembroke College
    (Cambridge), 35
Penn, William, 110, 151
Pepys, Samuel, 26, 93
Pepys Library, 26
Persuasion (Austen), 11
Peterhouse College
    (Cambridge), 36
Pickerel pub, 26
Pierrepont Place, 7
Plantagenet Restaurant,
    146, 149
Poetry Bookshop, 81
Popjoys Restaurant, 10
Prebendal School, 52
prehistoric earthworks,
    70–71, 75–76
Pryll Cottage, 62
pubs
    Bath, 8, 15
    Cambridge, 24, 26, 34
    Canterbury, 46
    Chichester, 57
    Church Stretton, 63
    Hay-on-Wye, 82, 84
    Oxford, 111
    Salisbury, 131, 132
    Solva, 118, 120, 121
    Stow-on-the-Wold,
        137–38
    Tenby, 144
    Wells, 157
    York, 171–72

Pulteney Bridge, 6, 15
Pump Room, 8
punting, 34, 106–7

Quant, Mary, 14
Quay Hill, 146
Queen Elizabeth's Guest
    Chamber, 43
Queens' College (Cam-
    bridge), 34–35
Queen's College (Ox-
    ford), 103, 105–6
Queens' Hall, 35

Radcliffe Camera, 99
Ragleth House, 64
Rectory Field, 65
Rees, Thomas ap, 146
Residentiary, 53
restaurants
    Bath, 10, 12
    Chichester, 52, 53
    Dorchester, 72, 73
    Tenby, 146, 149
    see also pubs
Reynolds, Sir Joshua, 22,
    93, 103, 110
Rhodes, Cecil, 111
Richard III, King, 164
Risam, William, 146
River Alun, 114, 116
River Avon, 6, 130, 131–
    32
River Cam, 26
River Dikler, 139
River Foss, 169
River Frome, 67, 74
River Nadder, 132
River Stour, 40
Roman artifacts
    Bath, 8, 9–10
    Canterbury, 43–44
    Chichester, 49, 51, 56
    York, 159, 162
Roman baths, 8, 9–10

Roman emperors (busts), 98
Roman Museum, 43–44
Roman roads, 133
Romney, George, 110
Round Church, 27
Royal Crescent, 13
Royalist Hotel, 137–38, 140
Royal Lion pub, 144
Royal Mineral Water Hospital, 15
Rubens, Peter Paul, 33

Sackville family. See Knole House
Sackville-West, Vita, 88
Sadler, James, 108
St. Augustine's marble chair, 45
St. Brides Bay, 123
St. Catherine's College (Cambridge), 35
St. Catherine's island, 145
St. David's, 113, 114–18
  Bishop's Palace, 114, 116–17
  cathedral, 118
  map of, 115
  Old Cross hotel, 118, 123
  tourist information, 123
  transportation to, 113
St. Edmund Hall, 103–4
St. Edward's House, 136
St. John's Chapel, 23
St. John's College (Cambridge), 24, 25, 27
St. John's garden, 23
St. Lawrence, church of, 64–65
St. Leonard's Hospital, 162

St. Mary's Abbey, 159
St. Mary's Church, 146
St. Mary's Hospital, 57
St. Peter's Church, 72
St. Thomas's Church, 131
St. Thomas's Hospital, 43
St. William's College, 164
Salisbury, 124–32
  art in public places, 128, 130
  Bridge Street, 131
  churches, 124, 125, 128–30, 131
  cloisters, 130
  High Street, 131
  houses of historic interest, 130–31
  map of, 126–27
  Minster Street, 131
  museums, 129–30
  Poultry Cross, 131
  pubs, 131, 132
  Silver Street, 131
  transportation to, 125
Salisbury Cathedral, 124, 125, 128–30
Saracen's Head pub, 15
Senate House, 30–31
Sevenoaks, 87, 89
Seymour, Thomas, Earl of Hertford, 128–29
Shannon, Lady, 92
Sheila na Gig ("Sheila of the breasts") statues, 64–65
Sheldonian Theatre, 99
Ship Hotel, 55–56, 57
Ship Inn, 120
Shire Hall, 73–74
Sidney Sussex College (Cambridge), 27–28
Silver Tissue Dress, 14
Smalls, the (reef), 121
Smith, Captain John, 129

Solva, 113, 118–23
  Coast path, 122–23
  lighthouses, 121–22
  map of, 119
  Non-Conformist chapel, 120
  pubs, 118, 120, 121
  tourist information, 123
  transportation to, 113
Star pub, 157
Still, Bishop, 154
Stow-on-the-Wold, 133–40
  churches, 136, 139–40
  Church Street, 136
  Digbeth Street, 137
  history of, 133, 136
  hotels, 137–38, 140
  houses of historic interest, 136, 138, 139
  maps of, 134, 135
  Park Street, 138
  pubs, 137–38
  Sheep Street, 138
  tourist information, 140
  Union Street, 138
  Well Lane, 138
Strafford, Earl of, 162
Stuart dynasty, 163
sundials, 25, 35
Sun Hotel, 46
Sutherland, Graham, 51–52
Swan at Hay (hotel), 85

Tenby, 141–49
  art galleries and museums, 148–49
  beaches, 144
  Bridge Street, 147
  castles, 148
  Castle Square, 147

churches, 146
Cob Lane, 146
gardens, 146
harbor area, 147
history of, 141, 144
hotels, 145, 149
houses of historic
    interest, 146–48
map of, 142–43
the Paragon, 146
pubs, 144
restaurants, 146, 149
St. Julian's Street, 146
tourist information,
    149
transportation to, 144
Warren Street, 144
White Lion Street, 144
Tenby Museum, 148
Tess of the D'Urbervilles
    (Hardy), 70
Theatre Royal, 162
theaters
Bath, 7
Chichester, 56
Oxford, 99
York, 162
Three Tuns pub, 82
Tiger Hall, 65
Tolpuddle Martyrs, 73
Tompion, Thomas, 8
Tom Tower, 108, 109
Tower of the Five
    Orders, 100
Town and Gown (pub),
    24
Town Hall (Hay-on-
    Wye), 83
Treasurer's House, 165
Trim Bridge, 10
Trinity Bridge, 23
Trinity Chapel, 45
Trinity College (Cam-
    bridge), 20–23
Tudor Cottage, 64

Tudor Merchant's
    House, 146–47
Tudor Tower, 27
Tumpy Field, 85

University Library (Cam-
    bridge), 23
Upper Slaughter, 139

Vicars' Hall (Wells), 157
Vicars' Hall and Under-
    croft (Chichester),
    53
Viking Centre, 171

Wales. *See* Hay-on-Wye;
    St. David's; Solva;
    Tenby
Weavers, The (house), 43
Wells, 150–57
    art in public places, 154
    Bishop's Palace, 155–
        56
    Cathedral Green, 157
    churches, 151, 154–55
    clock towers, 154
    gardens, 156
    map of, 152–53
    Market Place, 150–51
    museums, 157
    Penniless Porch, 151
    pubs, 157
    St. Andrew Street,
        156, 157
    tourist information,
        157
    transportation to, 150
    Vicars' Close, 156–57
Wells Museum, 157
Wenlock Edge, 58
Westgate Gardens, 42
Westgate House, 40
Westgate Museum, 41
White Hart pub, 138
Whitesands Bay, 117

Whiteside, Henry, 121,
    122
Whyting, Richard, 156
William of Orange, 10
Wolfe, General James, 10
Wolsey, Cardinal Thomas,
    106, 109, 110
Wood, John, the Elder,
    10, 13
Wood, John, the
    Younger, 12, 14
Wordsworth, William, 6
workhouses, 138
Wrekin, The, 66
Wren, Sir Christopher,
    23, 35, 99, 109, 129
Wren Library, 23

Ye Olde Starre Inn, 171–
    72
York
    art galleries and
        museums, 163
    art in public places,
        165–66
    churches, 165–66,
        167, 168, 171
    College Street, 164
    Coppergate, 171
    first walk, 158–59,
        162–66
    gardens, 159
    High Petergate, 167
    hospitals, 162
    houses of historic
        interest, 162–63,
        165, 168, 171
    King's Court, 168
    Kings Square, 168
    libraries, 162
    Low Petergate, 167
    map of, 160–61
    museums, 159, 164,
        170
    Piccadilly, 169

York (*cont'd*)
    pubs, 171–72
    ramparts, 163–64
    Roman artifacts, 159,
      162
    St. Helen's Square, 171
    St. Leonard's Place, 162

    second walk, 167–72
    the Shambles, 168
    Stonegate, 167, 171
    theaters, 162
    tourist information,
      172
    transportation to, 159

    Viking Centre, 171
    Whip-Ma-Whop-Ma-
      Gate, 169
York Minster, 165–66
Yorkshire Museum, 159
Yorvik Viking Centre,
    171